100 Years of Vintage Watches

Dean Judy

Published by

krause publications

700 East State Street • Iola, WI 54990-0001
715/445-2214 • FAX: 715/445-4087   www.krause.com

Please call or write for our free catalog of publications. Our toll-free number to place an order or obtain a free catalog is (800) 258-0929.

Library of Congress Catalog Number: 2002105749
ISBN: 0-87349-453-9

Acknowledgments

I would like to first of all thank my beautiful wife and best friend, Kristy, for her creative support, hard work, and encouragement. Very special thanks go out to Eric Iskin, Bill Hegner, and Rene Rondeau for their generous help and sharing of their watch-collecting experience. Many thanks to Mary Huff of the American Watchmakers-Clockmakers Institute for technical research help. Thanks to Margaret Judy for her help with editing and Dan Judy for his imaging work.

A warm thank you to the National Association of Watch and Clock Collectors members and fellow watch enthusiasts, who allowed me to photograph their watches: George Roberts, Doyle Cogburn, Fred and Lisa Cooper, Kurt Rothner, Don Levison, Gregg Esses, Armand Gandara, Lance Thomas, Don Allen, Mark Smith, Paul Yu, Brad Johnson, Jim Griggs, Harry Butler, Bill White, Eric Iskin, Bill Hegner, and Rene Rondeau.

I would like to acknowledge the following watch companies of Switzerland for their generous assistance: Blancpain, Jaeger-LeCoultre, Longines, Mido, Movado, Ulysse Nardin, Omega, Rado, and Tissot.

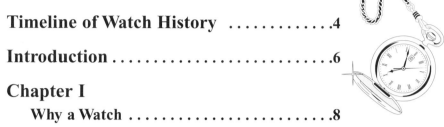

Table of Contents

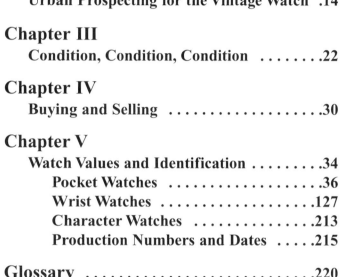

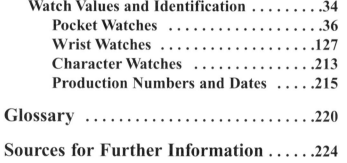

Timeline of Watch History

1880s Swiss companies realize they cannot compete by using old methods of hand making each watch and begin to develop mass-production techniques.

1900s Inexpensive non-jeweled "dollar watches," being produced in large numbers, start gaining in popularity and market share.

1870s American watch companies perfect mass production by inventing new machinery, innovative production methods, and the use of interchangeable parts. Key winding and key setting is gradually replaced with stem winding and stem setting watches.

1890s Newly instituted Railroad Standards challenge American watch companies. The result is the highest quality, mass-produced timepieces in the world.

1910s 16-size railroad grade production peaks. Wrist watches are introduced into the market by many manufacturers.

1920s Swiss wrist watches are imported into America in huge quantities. Increased numbers of smaller, 12-size pocket watches are being produced.

1940s Military precision demands unadorned, rugged timepieces. Pocket watch production declines. Increased numbers of self-winding watches are produced.

1960s Bulova Accutron tuning-fork watch produced. Ultra-thin watches and scratchproof crystals emerge. Omega chronograph lands on the moon.

1930s Styles and shapes of wrist watches go through beautiful Art-Deco period. Pocket watches get slimmer and smaller.

1950s Styles, shapes, mechanical, and technical innovations go wild. Electric watches appear on the market. American watch companies are in final decline.

1970s Quartz watches explode in popularity worldwide as mechanical watch production declines. Swiss watch industry loses market share to Japan. Collecting of the mechanical watch begins in earnest.

Introduction

Circa 1910 poster of god "Chronos." Courtesy of Omega Watch Co.

Hello! Welcome to the fascinating world of vintage watch collecting. The search for, and the collecting of, these miniature jeweled time machines is a wondrous journey full of fun, excitement, discovery, profit, and knowledge. This book will guide you through the 100-year period from the 1870s to the 1970s. In it you will find a great cross-section of pocket watches, wrist watches, and watch memorabilia from this fabulous watch-making period.

What is a vintage watch? Generally speaking, anything made before 1960 is considered to be "vintage." Anything made before 1920 is considered to be "antique." I, however, don't subscribe to any strict lines of distinction and have chosen the arbitrary cutoff date to a "vintage" watch as any watch that was made before the advent of the LCD (liquid crystal diode) quartz, battery-powered timepiece.

The quartz watch started taking over the market in the 1970s, but there are still some extremely collectible mechanical (wind-up) watches to be found from this decade that are very desirable. Quartz watches ruled the market after the 1970s and still represent the vast majority of timepieces being produced today. The quartz watch—highly marketed early on by Texas Instruments and Seiko—nearly drove the Swiss watch industry to its knees, and took away the huge market share it had enjoyed for decades. Interestingly enough, it was the Swiss who invented the quartz technology, but at first they ignored it. Fortunately, they regrouped, joined in, and saved themselves by coming out with watches like the "Swatch Watch." Today, the finest and most valuable watches are still produced in Switzerland, and are mechanical—manual wind and automatic wind—timepieces, not quartz.

The later half of the 1800s and early part of the 1900s were high times for watch manufacturing, especially in America, and I consider watches from this period as vintage also. To me, a "vintage" watch is one that can be worn and enjoyed, even if it is only on special occasions. On the other hand, an "antique" watch is one I consider being so fragile and old that it must remain at rest in a display case somewhere. The 100 years from the 1870s to the 1970s, the period of watch collecting that I love the best, took us from the "turnip"—a large, rounded pocket watch—to high-tech space-age marvels worn on the wrist.

In this book, I will review some history of watch making and collecting, offer tips on searching for watches, help you understand how to ascertain the condition of vintage watches, and give you buying and selling tips. Values and prices, and a photo gallery of watches and memorabilia, are also featured. Also, I provide useful addresses and contacts for further expanding your knowledge on the subject. For those of you just starting out in search of a vintage watch, I do hope this book will provide a spark that ignites a passion inside you to study, learn, and appreciate the wonderful world of horology—the study of the art and science of time, timekeeping, and timekeepers. For those seasoned watch lovers who are reading this, I do hope you find a helpful tip or two inside these pages that may open up other avenues to your searching and add to the pleasure of discovering just one more beautiful miniature machine.

My interest in the world of watches started back in 1975 when I served as an apprentice to a master watchmaker. My short-lived apprenticeship was enough to spark a lifelong interest in watches, horology, and all the memorabilia connected with it. The folks who owned the "mom and pop" jewelry store could not afford to pay me much and sadly, after one short year, I had to leave for a higher-paying job to support my young family. It was the only job I've ever had, though, that I couldn't wait to get up in the morning and go to. There were three old gentlemen in the back room and a wonderful lady in the front who had well over 125 years combined experience in the watch and jewelry world. I was like a young sponge, soaking up all the knowledge and history that they would impart.

My interview for the position was a brief one. After a short introduction, the owner and master watchmaker, Tom Locke, handed me a watchband, a spring bar, and an old wrist watch. He said, "Put that band on the watch," then folded his arms and leaned back to see how I would do. I had messed around with putting an old broken watch band back together in the past, and so had some idea as to what to do. In no time at all, I had the spring bar into the band and the band placed between the lugs of the timepiece. After starting one end in a hole, I used my thumbnail to gingerly compress the bar and snap it home into the remaining hole in the watch lug. I handed it back to him. He glanced over to his wife, Roberta, looked back to me and said, "You're hired. The last guy we had in here had hands like a bear cub, and couldn't do that little procedure." So started my lifelong love of watches and their histories. In the months that followed, I learned how to first examine watches, remove the movements from their cases, polish the cases and crystals, and eventually disassemble, clean, repair, and reassemble the jeweled movements themselves.

The first few days in the repair shop I just watched, listened, and learned. We placed a running movement under a microscope and I watched for hours in amazement as the tiny wheels whirled and oscillated, gears turned and meshed, and the mainspring released its power to eventually drive the hands around so one could read the passing of time. I vowed to myself, then and there, that if some mechanical wizard could actually design, create, assemble, and make this thing work, I would at least learn how to take it apart and put it back together again, without totally screwing it up in the process. Mr. Locke told me to go slow—very slow. "Don't rush," he said. "Speed will come later." No boss that I ever had before, or since, told me to work slowly. I liked that. It should be the same for you if you are just starting out. Go slowly at first in the learning and handling of fine watches. Take your time to learn the art of observation. Be patient and open up all of your senses while you are learning about, searching, and researching the exciting world of watches. One of the most wonderful benefits of my many years of working with watches has been the learning of "being here now." Pushing yourself to be in the present moment fully and totally, while handling one of these precious little machines, will help reduce the chances of dropping it, breaking it, smashing its tiny gears and wheels, and other abuses.

It is my desire, within the pages of this book, to impart to you a portion of knowledge, great watch photographs, watch values, stories of the search, lessons I've learned, and some "tips of the trade." I have attempted to keep it brief and to the point without loading you down with too many facts and figures, and just give you the "meat" of the subject matter. Please remember as you search for watch treasures to enjoy the journey. The destination will draw you.

Dean Judy

February 2002

What makes it tick?

A Norman Rockwell ad, "It's Watch Inspection Time."

Why A Watch

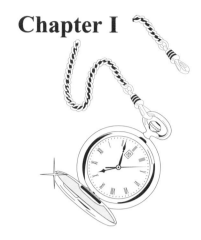

Chapter I

"I've got all the time in the world." I often repeat this little saying to myself when feeling squeezed for time in this fast-paced life of our 21st century. This always slows me down a bit and helps me focus on just enjoying the journey.

It has been said that time is irrelevant and, in eternity, does not even exist. Well, time may not be important in other dimensions, but it sure is in this one. I have met a number of people who tell me, "I hate watches. I don't even wear one." These same people will always be running late, trying to make some appointment and asking strangers, "Please, can you tell me the time?" When someone asks for the time and you glance down at your watch and tell them, you have just shared a bit of knowledge, a tiny piece of scientific wizardry. Of course, you can then come back with, "Do you know what time it really is?" They will stare questioningly into your eyes and then you say, "It's time you bought a watch, buddy!"

So saying, if you've got to have a watch, why not own a really cool one like a red LED (light-emitting-diode) wrist watch out of the early 1970s that someone like Darth Vader would have on. Or maybe a lady's Art Deco Gruen Curvex from the 1930s, or a man's Hamilton 992B pocket watch. How about high-stepping with a 1950's Rolex on your wrist. Why not own a watch that is special so that every time you look at it, it's fun and it gives you pleasure?

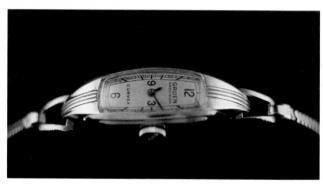

Gruen, ladies Curvex, circa 1930s.

Rolex Submariner, circa 1950s.

Pulsar LED, Time Computer Inc. USA, circa 1970s.

Hamilton RR, 992B, circa 1942.

Omega, Speedmaster Professional, three-register Chronograph, circa 1966 (pre-moon).

NASA astronauts who venture out into space know the importance of their "mechanical" watches. If all electric computer systems should fail, their lives could depend on the timepiece on their wrists. This actually happened in 1970 during the Apollo 13 mission when the crew had to rely on their Omega Speedmaster Professional Chronograph to time the rocket burn that got them safely back to earth after an on-board explosion disaster.

Vintage watch collecting is so enjoyable because the collectible can be used in your daily life. Your collectible doesn't have to just sit around acquiring layers of dust. It can be worn, looked at, listened to, and shown off every day. Watches are great conversation pieces and perform useful functions.

Measuring Time

No one person can be found who is responsible for the invention of the watch. It is believed that the first watches gradually started appearing around the end of the 1400s and the beginning of the early 1500s. These were actually small clocks made to be portable. The clocks of the time were stationary and all driven by weights. This form of power was not practical for a portable clock (watch), so the use of spring tension was developed and expanded upon by metalsmiths and clockmakers. Spring (mainspring) driven clocks were scaled down further and further by these craftsmen, clockmakers, jewelers, metalsmiths, inventors, etc., and the portable watch gradually came into being. Watches were first made for the very wealthy aristocrats, princes, kings, queens, and the like.

During the 1600s, extremely beautiful watches were created in France, England, Switzerland, and Germany, many of which survive today in museums and private collections. During the next two centuries, the art of watchmaking and casemaking was improved upon and perfected. Through many inventions and innovations, watches became more durable and accurate timepieces. Early European master watchmakers and inventors, from the 1600s, 1700s, and 1800s, such as Christian Huygens, Thomas Tompion, George Graham, John Harrison, Thomas Mudge, Julien and Pierre LeRoy, Jean-Antoine Lepine, and

Abraham-Louis Breguet, were minds instrumental in perfecting the mechanics of watches. Watch case artisans in Switzerland, like Jean-Jacques Rousseau and the Huaud brothers, created enameled and hand-painted works of art, decorating watch cases used all over Europe. The early pocket watch dial (face) was made of metal, usually engraved, and highly decorated. Later on, the white enamel dial became the most common.

The early watchmakers in America fabricated their watches mostly from parts made overseas and imported into the country. Not until around the 1850s did Americans start producing watches completely made in this country. Famous companies such as The American Watch Company of Waltham, Massachusetts, and E. Howard & Co. of Boston, Massachusetts, were the first really big concerns to take off, supplying Americans with quality timepieces. Many watch companies followed: the New Haven Clock and Watch Co., New Haven, Connecticut; National Watch Co. (Elgin Watch Co.), Elgin, Illinois; Illinois Watch Co., Springfield, Illinois; Rockford Watch Co., Rockford, Illinois; Columbus Watch Co., Columbus, Ohio; Hampden Watch Co., Canton, Ohio; Ball Watch Co., Cleveland, Ohio; Waterbury Watch Co., Waterbury, Connecticut; Seth Thomas Watch Co., Thomaston, Connecticut; U.S. Watch Co., Waltham, Massachusetts; New York Standard Watch Co., Jersey City, New Jersey; Trenton Watch Co., Trenton, New Jersey; Wesclox, Athens, Georgia; Ingersoll (Robert H. Ingersoll & Bros.), New York, New York; Hamilton Watch Co., Lancaster, Pennsylvania; South Bend Watch Co., South Bend, Indiana; and E. Ingraham Co., Bristol, Connecticut. These were just some of the larger American watch companies. There were many smaller watch manufacturing companies that produced watches for a time and then, for varying reasons, went out of business. There were well more than 300 million watches produced by these U.S. companies, plus millions more imported into this country from Switzerland. Many of these vintage watches have survived to this day and are lying around somewhere just waiting to be discovered.

In this book, I am focusing on vintage watches from the years after the Civil War, for it was in this time period that the modern "stem winding and stem setting" mechanism gradually came into more common use.

Keywind pocket watch movement, Switzerland.

Using a "watch key" to wind the mainspring and set the time (hands) on your watch was the way it was done prior to this invention. Having to take care of a key for your watch is a bit of a hassle. Although it is quaint and can be fun to wind your watch with a key, keys get misplaced and, if you're not careful, they can scratch your watch if you're in a hurry to wind or set your timepiece. Many early pocket watches were wound from the back and the hands were set from the front of the piece. I have seen many wonderful old watch dials chipped, and a few watch movements with skid marks from an errant watch key. One slip and you've messed up your neat old pocket watch. These antique "key wind-key set" watches are very cool to own and enjoy, but I have relegated them to the "fragile antique" category and focus on timepieces that can be carried and worn on a more daily basis.

The modern stem winding and setting system was perfected in Switzerland in the 1840s and gradually all watches eventually used it. However, key-wind watches were still being produced well into the late 1800s. So, in this watch guide, I will be guiding you, the collector, to watches made from approximately the 1870s, when stem winding (pendant set and wound) watches really started to take over the market, up to the 1970s when the quartz watch came roaring upon the scene.

Keywind pocket watch movement, American.

In America, as the early watch manufacturers poured more and more watches into the market, the prices for them gradually went down and the average person could eventually afford to own one. Still, the watch purchase usually represented a good deal of money, so the timepiece was often treasured and taken very good care of. It became more than an investment; it became an heirloom that could be passed down to other members of the family. To inherit your father's watch or one from your grandparents was, and still is, a very popular tradition. Watches became symbols of accomplishment and were given as rewards for reaching milestones in one's life, such as graduation, accomplishing career goals, and company retirement.

As the manufacturers competed with one another, they produced increasingly better watches, with more quality and beauty going into their movements and cases. The watch companies started decorating their movements with what is called "damaskeening" (Damascene: from the word Damascus). This was a decorative etching engraved into the metal plates and bridges of the movements during the final machining processes. This artwork had nothing to do with the functioning of the watch, but added a beauty and a special quality to the American pocket watch. Also, watch case companies were very competitive and so produced a wide variety of very ornately engraved cases. The cases had such things as birds, deer, flora, fauna, trains, and idyllic country scenes engraved on their outsides. These watch cases were made in solid gold, gold filled (base metal, usually brass, sandwiched between thick plates of gold), rolled gold plated (base metal with a very thin plating of gold), gold gilded (microns of gold chemically plated to the surface of base metal), silver, and silveroid (nickel silver—a silvery colored, hard, corrosion-resistant alloy of zinc, copper, and nickel). American pocket watches from this era are huge collectibles because of the machining precision and artwork put into their creation.

A whole book could easily be written on the subject of watch movements, their design, function, and evolution. I will just attempt to keep it simple for now, and talk about size and jeweling. The size of a watch is measured by the dimensions of the movement in either the Swiss ligne (ligne = 1/12 of a French inch), or the English and American size (measured in 1/30 of an English inch). To determine size, the movement is measured across the "dial" side of the main—sometimes called lower or pillar—plate. The gauge (on P. 11) gives you the different graduations of the "ligne" and the American "size." Sometimes it can be a bit tricky judging the size of a watch when looking at it cased. You have to picture the movement below the bezel, crystal, and dial. With enough practice handling the different sizes, you soon get a feel for what their real measure (size) is. Throughout this book, I will be mentioning the different sizes and, by using the gauge pictured, you will get the idea. For instance, the vast majority of American men's-sized pocket watches were 18 size (18" x 1/30" = 1-23/30" or approximately 1-3/4" diameter), 16 size (16" x 1/30" = 1-21/30" or approximately 1-11/16" diameter), or 12 size

(12" x 1/30" = 1-17/30" or approximately 1-9/16" diameter).

Gauge for measuring American movements (actual size).

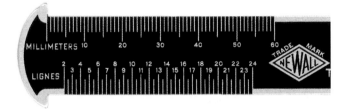

Gauge for measuring Swiss movements (actual size).

Jeweling, or the jewels used in watch movements, act as bearings. Let us say you drill a small hole into a brass plate and place the end (pivot) of a steel shaft into it. OK, now in the middle of the steel shaft rests a wheel-shaped piece of brass with teeth cut into the outside edge. Then you drill another small hole into another brass plate, and place it on the opposite end of the steel shaft that has the wheel in the middle of it. As the steel shaft and wheel spin round and round over years and years, eventually the harder steel wears into the softer brass and makes the hole bigger. Now the shaft has play in it, is loose fitting, and starts to wobble. Picture many such shafts with wheels and gears spinning around and getting wobbly. Soon, the whole affair would all come to a grinding halt, wouldn't it? Let's do it better, shall we? Now, you drill a small hole into a brass plate, but this time make it a bit larger so we can press into the hole a "doughnut"-shaped jewel. The end of your steel shaft, with the wheel on it, now fits into the "doughnut" hole in the middle of the jewel. Your steel shaft can spin around for centuries and centuries and not make the jewel hole larger or the shaft size smaller, providing you have lubrication.

This is, very basically, how the jewel functions inside the movement of a watch. The jewels are made from man-grown corundum (synthetic ruby and sapphire), and polished into the various shapes used for watchmaking. Therefore, one can readily see that the higher the jewel count in a watch, the higher the grade of precision and durability. The more jewels fitted into a watch at the factory, the more time spent on its manufacture and adjustments. Look at your basic 17-jewel watch like you would a car with a V-8 engine in it. A seven-jewel watch might be likened to a car with a 4-cylinder engine, a 15-jewel watch similar to a car with a V-6, and a 21-jewel watch like a high performance V-12 engine. In the 1930s and 1940s, more and more watches started appearing on the market equipped with spring-like settings holding the endstone (cap) jewels, or the endstones and jewel holes of the balance. These jewels would "give" when the watch received a shock, thus preventing the end (pivot) of the balance staff from breaking. Earlier watches were built well, especially the beefy pocket watches, but an accidental drop or shock to the movement would break even the best balance staff. With the invention of the many styles of shock-resistant jewel settings (Incabloc style pictured), broken balance staffs became, for the most part, a thing of the past.

Enlarged display of Incabloc style shock absorber system.

In 1891, there was a large train wreck near Kipton, Ohio. It was surmised that the watch of one of the train engineers had malfunctioned. One train was supposed to pull to a side track to let the other go by, but due to the pocket watch time-keeping problem, they were on the same track at the same time, and it resulted in a disastrous head-on collision.

After this wreck, local railroad officials asked Webb C. Ball, a Cleveland jeweler, to organize a standard system of checking timepieces. In time, many other railroads followed the standards set up by Webb C. Ball. These were standards that the watch manufacturers had to meet before railroads would approve their watches for railroad use. The watch companies were up to the task, and so began the production of the finest mass-produced, factory-made watches in the world. The American railroad grade and railroad approved watches were the "high tech" machines of their time, and still remain to this day as excellent and well-made timekeepers. They are, by far, the most popular American collectible pocket watches. The standards were very stringent and required that a pocket watch be as follows:

• American-made 16- or 18-size movements

• 17 jewels minimum

•Open face, with the stem at 12 o'clock to preclude a hunting movement in an open case

•Lever escapement with double roller and steel escape wheel

•Equipped with overcoil hairspring and micrometer regulator

•Adjusted for temperature, isochronism, and at least five positions

•Lever setting

•Accurate to 30 seconds per week, and reset to correct time whenever the error exceeded 30 seconds

•Cleaned annually and inspected every two weeks, with performance noted on a card carried by the trainman

•Mounted in a dust-tight case

•Equipped with a crystal free of chips and scratches

•Equipped with a dial of Arabic numerals, heavy style hands, a second hand, and minute divisions

THE Hamilton Watch

HAMILTON

THE RAIL ROAD TIMEKEEPER OF AMERICA.

LANCASTER, PA.

Hamilton Watch Co. ad.

Railroad pocket watches had to keep time in at least five different positions, such as when laying dial-side down, laying dial-side up, stem-up position, stem-left position, and stem-right position, that were adjusted to temperatures so as to keep time whether you were in Alaska or Florida. They have a lever to set the hands to prevent the hands from accidentally being moved while carrying the timepiece in your watch pocket. Unlike pulling out on the crown/stem to turn the hands for setting, a true railroad watch must have a lever you pull out, after removing the bezel/crystal, to then engage the setting mechanism. These were some of the early standards set up, and as the years passed, there were additions and other requirements. Today, many railroad watch collectors look for the 21- and 23-jewel timepieces in the 18 and 16 size.

During the 1920s and 1930s, as wrist watches started taking over the market, watch manufacturers produced slimmer and smaller pocket watches. There were many different shapes and beautiful Art-Deco styles produced during this period. The wrist watch really started gaining popularity in the late 1910s and early 1920s. In the early days, men thought wrist watches were a bit feminine and were slow to strap one on their wrist. During World War I, however, many men saw the practicality of having the time on one's wrist. Railroad men kept on carrying their pocket watches, but as the automobile slowly replaced the train as the preferred mode of transportation, so then did the wrist watch replace the pocket watch in popularity. It has been said that wrist watches were manufactured in the later part of the 1800s as the Swiss were experimenting with their use, but I personally have never seen one from this time period. I have, however, seen many small pocket watches that were converted over to be used on the wrist, and, in fact, this is how many watch companies entered into wrist-watch production.

The first wrist watches used small, round pocket-watch movements. As the competition ramped up among the manufacturers, different shaped wrist watches started to come out. In the later part of the 1920s and on into the 1930s, watch companies really went wild. In order to produce radically shaped wrist watches, watchmakers had to design different shaped movements. Using the standard round movements limited the design range. Companies came out with rectangular-shaped movements, rectangular with cut corners, oval shaped, barrel shaped, curved movements, and many variations. The round movement, though, by far, was and still remains to this day, the most popular and functional shape used. Watch dials, too, came in a variety of shapes, colors, textures, and different materials. Glass crystals were always used to protect the faces of the watches. These also started being produced in various shapes, colors, and thicknesses, and even facets were placed into their designs.

Shipping tin for dials, circa 1940s.

As modern men and women traveled the world in airplanes and fast automobiles, the watch companies made sure they could time their adventures with more accuracy. Wrist chronometers and chronographs were produced to measure time to the split second. The watch company of Rolex came out with a waterproof "Oyster" watch. Blancpain made the first early automatic "self winding" wrist watch prototype movements for Harwood watches. Longines watch company worked with Charles Lindbergh to create an aviator's watch. Watches were made radically curved to fit on the side of an automobile driver's wrist, so one could just glance over to read the time without moving the wrist. Fashion was ever changing, and so, too, were watch styles to keep pace. The 1930s produced beautiful Art Deco designs in wrist watches. In the 1940s, military watches were made dark, sturdy, plain, and reliable. Watches were produced for the global traveler to be easily adjusted to the different time zones. Wrist watches came out with built-in alarm mechanisms to wake you up or to remind you of an appointment. The 1940s also saw the end to pocket watch popularity and a rapid decline in their production.

In the 1950s, scuba diving became popular, with Jacques Cousteau leading the pace. Firms like Blancpain and Rolex created watches to withstand deep-sea pressures. As the jet and space ages came into being, watch houses like Omega and Breitling produced complicated professional watches to time missions and calculate speed and fuel consumption. In the late 1950s, the first electric watch came out from the Hamilton Watch Company. The 1960s produced the Accutron by Bulova. The 1970s brought about the short-lived popularity of the LED quartz watch. This is the time when I became a watchmaker apprentice. I worked at Locke's Village Jewelers in Santa Rosa, California. Tom Locke, the owner and master watchmaker, had filled his store with the "new fangled" Seiko quartz LCD (liquid crystal display) watches, and the typical analog quartz watches. There were a few red LED (light-emitting-diode) watches still in stock, but customers would come in and want to throw their LED watch they had purchased a year or two earlier at someone because the "batteries need to be replaced every six months!"

These early LED watches required two separate batteries to power and light them up. In order to tell the time on one of these "Darth Vader" specials, you had to press a button. Still, they were pretty cool and companies like Pulsar, Bulova, Longines, Omega, and Fairchild produced some really neat looking ones. Since they sucked the life out of early batteries (batteries are cheaper and better nowadays) and customers were always bringing them back, these watches were only produced for a few years.

All through these 100 years of watch production, high-end firms such as Audemars Puguet, Cartier, International Watch Company, Ulysse Nardin, Patek Philippe, Rolex, Tiffany & Company, and Vacheron Constantin, produced works of watchmaking art and mechanical excellence for the connoisseur and the wealthy. All of the aforementioned companies still exist today, but, alas, the American watch companies started vanishing when our country began importing millions of Swiss wrist watches in the 1920s and onward. The Great Depression spelled the end for some, but the big three—Hamilton, Waltham, and Elgin—managed to produce great watches well into the later part of the 1950s.

Urban Prospecting for the Vintage Watch

Chapter II

The Search

So, you've decided to start buying, selling, and yes, maybe even collecting a few vintage watches. Where do you begin? First, tell your friends and family members. Tell your Grandma, Grandpa, and all the senior citizens you know. Tell your co-workers and business associates. Tell anyone you know who knows a hundred other people. Then, kick back and wait.

Before you know it, you will be inundated with every style of (broken) Timex and cheap quartz watch, both men's and women's, ever made in the last 30 years. You'll receive bags of them, gobs of them. Don't be surprised if there are gooey ones with cake dough still imbedded in the back, and there will be smashed and crashed ones, watches that fell out of car windows and hit the pavement, ones with no crystals, crowns, or backs.

There will be watches with skid marks on them and ones impacted with every known (and unknown) kind of "people gunk" in every nook and cranny. Hey, don't complain—you can wash your hands later. There also might, just maybe, be a real nice vintage, jeweled, mechanical timepiece among the sandwich bags full of old watches that are bound to come to you, once you let the word out. These will be your practice watches.

There are many ways to search for vintage timepieces, all of which I have not discovered yet, but I have had luck with the following ways.

Classified Ads

Focusing your search can weed out the unwanted clunkers and cheaper "throw away" watches that come your way. In general, senior citizens have the lion's share of the vintage and antique watches that lie buried somewhere deep

A pile of old wrist watches.

in an old sock drawer long forgotten. Perhaps they stopped running and the owner decided they were not worth the hassle of fixing or servicing. Thankfully, for us urban prospectors, they were laid to rest by their owners and replaced by nifty $9.95 plastic quartz timepieces without souls. I run a continuous ad in a small local "Senior News" newspaper that comes out monthly. The secret is to keep the ad running month after month and, as people come across their old watches, your ad will come to mind. When they decide to part with a watch, chances are they will remember seeing your advertisement in the "Wanted" section of the classifieds and give you a call. Your ad might run like this: Watch collector seeks older mechanical (wind up) watches, working or not. Hamilton, Omega, Longines, Rolex, others. No Timex or Quartz. Please contact Bill Smith at 777-222-3333.

I have purchased many fine old timepieces from running ads like this one. I have also met some really great seniors and have had wonderful chats while reminiscing over a group of vintage watches. I am always polite and listen to their stories. It definitely helps to know some of the background and history of the watches you purchase, as you can pass this along to the future owners when you decide to resell them. Recently, I bought a couple of watches from a lady whose husband had passed away. One was a broken Swiss pocket watch he had brought back with him from Europe after World War II. On the back of this watch was engraved a winged railway car wheel on a section of railroad track, with the world and Swiss cross in the background. There was no name on the dial or movement, but the timepiece looks to have been made around the early 1920s and was probably used by a railroad worker. What an interesting story this watch could tell, from Swiss factory to railroad service, from traveling around Europe to ending up in an American GI's duffel bag, from sitting in a dresser drawer in Eureka, California, for 56 years, to ending up pictured in a vintage watch book (see top right photo on P. 39). Some day I will restore the pocket watch and send it on its merry way again. The other watch I purchased from this nice lady was the wrist watch her husband was wearing when she met him in the 1940s.

I do, however, recommend that you get as much information over the phone as you can. When someone first calls, take the time to ask them a few important questions. Ask if their watch (or watches) is a wind-up type watch, if that is what you're looking for. Ask if they can tell you what brand or who the maker of the watch is. Are they all men's watches? Ladies' watches? Can they tell you approximately how old the pieces are? Can they describe the overall condition to you as average, fine, or near mint? If you feel you have a good rapport with the caller, you might find out how much they are asking for the watch, so you can bring the appropriate amount of cash with you. What you are trying to establish by asking these questions is if you are going on a wild goose chase.

In my earlier days, I would take off from my house full of excitement and enthusiasm, drive clear across town on a cold, foggy night, and track down an elusive address in the dark, only to find a pile of worthless junk watches awaiting me. It didn't take too many of these dry runs before I figured out that I needed to qualify the caller, and their watches, with a basic line of preliminary questions. Many times these people will have other very collectible items that they want to sell, or they need information about some antique item. Recently, I got a call from a very nice older lady who had a few watches to show me. I went over to visit and ended up buying a vintage, non-working, 1920's Gruen wrist watch, and an original Gene Autry rug that she had purchased for her small son 53 years previously. The child's throw rug came complete with cowboy hat, Autry's signature, and a rope lariat all woven into it. I purchased the rug and the watch for a total of $20. You never know what you might bring home from a watch-prospecting search! I am not sure what I am going to do with the rug, but it is in great shape and definitely collectible.

I have been, what I now call, "urban prospecting" for vintage watches for more than 25 years. In my searching, I always keep an eye peeled for other cool collectible "old stuff," as I have met many wonderful people in my travels—people who collect everything from silver match safes to Evel Knievel lunch boxes, antique beads to vintage gasoline pumps, old advertising ashtrays with miniature rubber tires around them to heirloom jewelry with pavé diamonds, vintage musical instruments to antique barbed wire, old writing instruments to old Native American baskets, cool old 1940s' comic books to vintage cameras, autographs to phonographs, tools to toys, old coins to marbles, military memorabilia to 1960s' psychedelic posters—the list goes on and on. While I'm out rattling the bushes for old watches, I help other collectors by looking out for what they want. They, in turn, run across watch deals they pick up for me. It is great networking, for, as you know, one person's junk is another person's treasure. Down the road, I'll end up swapping the old Gene Autry rug to some other collector for a watch-related item.

I have also placed ads around the country in classified newspapers like the *Thrifty Nickel*, *The Nickel*, *Penny Saver*, Antiques and Collectibles newspapers, etc. If you have a computer online, you can go in and place inexpensive "watches wanted" ads in various cities all across America. The drawback with this type of search is that the seller has to describe the piece to you over the phone; you don't get to see it or listen to it, and they have to mail you the watch. A lot of trust from both the seller and you, the buyer, has to exist for a smooth transaction to take place. I generally tell the seller to mail me the item and I will pay for the postage. If I like the watch, I mail them a money order; if it's not at all what I thought it was going to be, I mail back the piece at no cost to the seller. Be sure you explain to them how to prepare it for shipping. Watches travel best when fully wound up, if they are in running condition, as they are more resistant to shock this way. Tell them to place a few inches of foam rubber, or bubble wrap, completely around the watch and ship it in a sturdy box marked "Fragile." You will need to ask many questions over the phone about the timepiece to avoid wasting each other's time mailing it back and forth across the country. I have never tried doing this in foreign newspapers yet, but I have purchased some rare vintage beauties in America this way.

Flea Markets

Flea markets are another wonderful place to find old watches. Some of my best finds have come from flea marts. I once told a slightly snobbish, retired jewelry store owner of my urban prospecting at flea markets. He laughed and said, "Do you really expect to find some great old Patek Philippe watch at some crummy flea market?" I answered back, "Well, I found a 1940s vintage Vacheron Constantin man's wrist watch at a flea market in this very town for $20, and from an antique dealer no less!" That got his attention.

Once, my wife Kristy and I went to a flea market just north of Santa Fe, New Mexico, where we were vacationing. I usually go around these flea markets asking every person who is selling antiques or collectibles if they have brought any old watches with them that day. Many of these dealers and vendors keep the good stuff hidden out of sight and only bring it out if someone asks or seems interested. Fine old watches and jewelry should not sit out on some card table baking in the sun all day. I asked to see an old "hunter case" pocket watch that was sitting in a glass case on a flea market table. It was a hot summer day in Santa Fe, and the lady whose table it was on opened the case and grabbed the watch. She couldn't hand it to me fast enough. "Yikes," she exclaimed. When I felt the watch in my hand, I immediately set it down on the table. It was so hot from the sun beating down on it through the glass of the showcase that a person couldn't hold it for two seconds. It was a very beautiful timepiece and I explained to her that the extreme heat was surely compromising the lubricating qualities of the minute amount of oil in the watch. I told her that the shellac holding the pallet jewels in place could soften and cause the jewels to move out of their proper position.

As I continued walking around inquiring about watches, another collector who had overheard me talking stopped me and let me know that I was wasting my time. He said that he had never seen any good timepieces at this flea market because the region had a lot of poor people living there and nobody ever owned good watches. I thanked him for the information and told him that I was having fun looking anyway. Not 10 minutes later, I was staring down at an old wooden table with a bunch of odds and ends on it. I noticed a couple of watches sitting there, and so inquired of the older gentleman whose table it was how much he was asking for the old wrist watches. He said $2 apiece, since they were not in the greatest condition, but he thought they were working. I asked if I could please see them. He handed them to me and I immediately recognized that one of them was a nice early 1960s automatic-wind

Swiss "Zodiac" watch with day, date, and moon phase complications. It was ticking. I told him I would take them, and walked away happy. He was also happy, as was my wife, when I sold the watch two weeks later and made a profit of $295. I don't remember what the other watches were that I bought with the Zodiac, but that one watch helped pay for the plane tickets on that vacation.

Don't forget to bring cards with you, with your name and number on them, to hand out to the dealers and vendors who left their "good watches" at home. Also, *get there early*. I cannot count the times when I've heard, "You're the fifth person to ask me about old watches this morning." Many times the regulars, who sell at these marts, keep watches they have come across in their travels between flea marts stashed away just to show to you when you come around, if it's one of the local affairs you frequent. They usually love to talk about how they came upon them and would rather sell them in a group to someone who is knowledgeable. They will pry you for information on what to look out for, what's hot, and what's not.

As I was writing this chapter, my wife and I went into the local town on the weekend and noticed they were having an indoor flea market that day. We pulled in and joined the treasure hunt. Sure enough, before long I came across a genuine Rolex watch box sitting on a table. It was a very large leather box with walnut wood lining inside. Unfortunately there was no watch inside, but I asked the young lady behind the table how much she wanted for it. She went over and asked her mom, returned to me and said, "Twenty dollars for the box." It was in great condition and approximately 20 years old. I asked if she would take $15 for it. Her mother overheard. "No way," she said. "Twenty dollars firm. Take a look on the bottom." I turned the box over and saw that she had placed a price tag of $45 on it. Well, I thought to myself, this lady knows she has a nice item and is offering it to me at a very fair price. I gladly gave her the $20 and thanked them both. One week later, this box sold for $127 on the Internet auction site eBay. Always pick up watch-related items like this if you find them in good condition and at reasonable prices, for you never know when you might run into another watch that the box would work great for. Keep an eye out for vintage watch bands, watchcases, parts or pieces, for they don't take up much room, and they always come in handy at some point for restoration purposes or "trading stock" to other urban watch prospectors.

Thrift Stores

Thrift stores, like the Salvation Army and Goodwill, are good places to check for vintage watches. At first, I was reluctant to go into these places because I figured all the good stuff was gleaned by the people in the back room or the members of the staff who went out and picked up the items at the collection points. However, old stuff attracts other old stuff, and sure enough, I have found good buys at these stores on occasion. Once, my wife Kristy suggested we check out the thrift store in the town we were traveling through. I was in one of my "I don't want to go into a thrift store" moods at the time and voiced my opinion that antiques shops would be a better choice. She talked me into it and dragged me inside a very large thrift store. I moped around for awhile, wishing we had gone into an antiques shop instead. Then I spotted a box full of watches. They were all plastic quartz types, but I halfheartedly poked around thinking that maybe I would find something I could use. Lo and behold, I came across a stainless-steel watch.

Examining my find closer revealed a vintage early 1970s Swiss Omega automatic "Cosmic" wrist watch in original condition. It had the original Omega leather band on it with the factory signed buckle still in place. It was not working. I asked a saleslady how much the watches were. She said $2 if they were working and $1 if they were not. I went to the checkout with my newly found treasure. The man there shook the watch, noticed it didn't work, and charged me $1 for it. When Kristy and I walked back to our car, she asked me if I had found anything while shopping. I said, "Yeah, I found $200 there in an old shoe box." "What?" she exclaimed. I showed her the Omega I had just bought for $1 and told her that when it was serviced and spruced up, it would fetch around $225 to $295. Needless to say, she brings that story up every time I balk at going into a thrift shop when we're out and about. That particular watch needed some expert repair work to get it back into proper running condition, but after I invested some time and money into it, I realized a profit of $190. I sold the watch to a gentleman in Switzerland who was the high bidder on the piece in an eBay auction I held.

Garage Sales

Of course, garage sales are also a great place for the intrepid urban prospector to find hidden treasures. If I don't see any older watches in a particular garage sale, I will always inform the person having the sale that I am interested in old-time, wind-up-type watches. Many times the people will have granddad's old railroad watch wrapped up in a sock somewhere in a dresser drawer. They won't even think to bring it out to a garage sale. Garage sale prices are also generally lower than flea market or thrift store prices.

Estate Sales

I have found bargains at estate sales, when family and friends run the sale. But, as a rule, if professionals are hired, they are usually aware of vintage and antique watch values. However, sometimes when there is to be a huge estate sale and there is just too much stuff, an old watch may not be researched thoroughly and may be under-priced. Of course, being there early helps in finding any deals. I was once invited to preview an estate sale the day before it was held because the person having it knew I was interested in watches. It just so happened that the gentleman, whose estate was being sold, was a part-time watch repairman/hobbyist. I was like a kid in a candy store! It is so nice to calmly go through boxes of nice old watch stuff,

and then consummate a deal with the sellers in a relaxed atmosphere—much better than a mad house affair where 75 people are milling around looking for buried treasure. If you contact the people who provide estate liquidation services, they can put you on their mailing list and keep you informed of upcoming estate sales where watches are present. They might even let you have the first look at them.

Auction Houses

Live auctions are also a place to find old watches of value. Most towns and all cities have auctioneers who hold auctions regularly. If you decide to attend an auction, be sure to give yourself plenty of time to preview the items up for auction, prior to the sale. But always remember— knowledge is power. One has to do their due diligence and study the subject of watch collecting. If you can glance at a box full of watches and know the approximate retail value of a particular piece, and know it to be 10 times the starting bid price, that is power and you can use it accordingly. Just don't get too hung up in the ego trip and excitement of having to best another bidder when the lot comes up and the bidding commences. You can end up with a handful of watches, having paid what amounts to a retail price, in a hot hurry.

Upscale auction houses, such as Sotheby's and Christie's, are very knowledgeable of the current values of timepieces, and in many cases, set the values for the market. You get to see nicer pieces, but the prices are higher. I am not an expert in this area, but if money is not an issue, these upscale auction houses are wonderful places to view fabulous vintage watches. In the past, I have been on their mailing lists and have received beautiful color brochures and booklets describing upcoming auctions of fine timepieces. These make wonderful reference materials, even if you can't make the auctions.

Antiques Shops

Antiques shops have been, for me, anyway, great places to find old watches. It is very hard to be an expert in everything out there that is collectible or has value as an antique, and antiques dealers only know so much about everything in their shops. I have found many a good and fair deal in antiques shops and collectives. Once, my friend and I were in an old shop poking around and admiring the wonderful array of items. This was one of those shops where everything was priced so high you wondered if the owner really wanted to sell anything or not. Every item we looked at was 20 to 40 percent higher than we figured it ought to be. It wasn't looking good for this urban watch prospector. In fact, I didn't even see any watches at all. My friend and I decided to leave, as the prices were just too depressing. On a whim, I stopped and asked the proprietor, who was sitting in a rocking chair, if he happened to have any old watches. He replied, "I hate watches. I sell them to customers and they're always bringing them back and telling me that they're not keeping perfect time." I told him it didn't matter to me if they ran or not, because I liked to restore them. He said he had a shoe box full of old watches in the back room and, if I bought them all, I could have them for $125. I was amazed. This was the last place on earth I had expected to find a deal. I walked out of there with more than a dozen different men's wrist watches from the 1930s, '40s, and '50s.

Antiques dealers also have connections with auctioneers, estate liquidators, junk dealers, and so on. If they know you are a serious buyer, they will keep their eyes open for you. Antiques collectives are an even greater resource for the urban prospector because there are so many dealers under one roof. In recent years, the cost of running an antiques store became too much for many dealers. So, dealers banded together to form collectives. They rented out different sized floor areas in their shops, and even rented out small glass showcase space. Some of these collectives are huge. There can be 50 different dealers selling merchandise in the same store and putting out old watches they've found.

The Internet

The Internet, as you probably already know, is huge. A person can spend days on the World Wide Web finding Web pages of people who deal in watches, auctions on watches, histories of watches, new watches, vintage watches, and so on. Most all of the watch companies, associations, watch collectors, and watch dealers who helped me with this book have Web sites on the Internet. There are also chat rooms where you can learn more about watch collecting and perhaps make a contact to track down a special watch or part. One of the biggest boons to watch lovers is eBay. On any given day, you can find in excess of 35,000 watches up for auction on this Internet auction site.

The following are some tips I've discovered while trying to uncover cyber watch deals. It all boils down to the search. When you go to eBay and type the word "watch" in the search title, you will come up with approximately 30,000 to 35,000 watch auctions at any given time. This is where most sellers and buyers go. If you enter the word "wristwatch" in the search title, you will get only around 1,000 to 1,500 auctions that come up. Congratulations! You have just stepped ahead of thousands of other urban prospectors out there searching for deals. Most people just enter the one word "watch" in their search, kick back, and see what is out there. The same goes for "pocketwatch." If you separate the word into two words, i.e., "pocket watch," a lot more auctions will come up than if you just put in the one word. On eBay, the secret is to find auctions that very few other watch prospectors have found.

I have, for instance, used the search term "Longine," instead of the more common spelling "Longines." I bought a very nice watch, at a very reasonable price, using the old Swiss spelling "chronographe" for a search term, instead of the correct spelling of "chronograph." I was bidding on this watch with virtually no competition. The seller in this instance did not use the word "watch" at all in his auction title description. He just listed it as "Old Swiss Chronographe." Try misspelling famous watch manufacturer's names, or try adding dashes, exclamation marks (i.e., watch- or watch!). Some people get all excited when writing up their watch auction and don't think to keep the word "watch" separate and totally by itself. Try using the search terms "watches," "pocketwatches," or "wristwatches," and see what comes up. You're going to places where 90 percent of the buyers don't go. Try words like "timekeeper" or "timepieces." It is fun to think up other oddball spellings or misspellings and quirky words people might use in their auction titles. I have purchased many a fine watch from Germany using the search terms "uhr," "uhren," and "armbanduhr." You can go to an Internet site translator, such as Altavista Babel Fish, and experiment with foreign terms for watch, wristwatch, etc., and then try them out in a search on eBay. It's a great way to learn some words in a foreign language and to connect with watch collectors internationally.

Also, the early bird gets the watches. Try searching for watch auctions that have just been recently listed, instead of the auctions just getting ready to end. You might be able to contact the seller and buy it early before 300 other vintage watch fans discover it. Or, if some night owl with insomnia lists their cool old watch at 3 a.m., you could be there at 3 a.m., when the auction ends. While everyone else is asleep at the wheel, you could be the last bidder on the auction. Watch collectors are famous for waiting until the last second of an auction to place their high bid.

eBay is not the only site on the Web to find vintage watches, so don't limit yourself. Sotheby's is a great place to discover beautiful watch auctions. It has a wide variety and you can always count on finding exotic and rare timepieces on its site. Christie's auction site is another wonderful place to visit for the urban prospector searching for treasures. There are many vintage watch enthusiasts who have their own Web sites online. They list their watches with many nice pictures and are more likely to stand behind what they sell. Many times, these individuals are watchmakers themselves, or have had their watchmaker service the timepieces they have for sale. When buying vintage watches from dealers who have their own sites, you are more apt to get a guarantee or a return policy on the watch, unlike some online auctions.

NAWCC Member decal.

The National Association of
Watch and Clock Collectors

The National Association of Watch and Clock Collectors, located in Columbia, Pennsylvania, is an excellent organization to belong to and I highly recommend you join. The knowledge you gain and contacts made from being a member are well worth the very low yearly dues you pay to join. The various chapters of the NAWCC hold regular local meetings and special regional events all over the country, and overseas as well. The organization also has a great Internet site to visit at www.nawcc.org. I have spent many wonderful days at marts, local meetings, and regional meets viewing collections, buying, participating in the silent auctions, selling watches and memorabilia, and expanding my knowledge by leaps and bounds. I could write an entire book on just these NAWCC adventures alone. Needless to say, the association functions are some of the best places for the urban watch prospector to hang out. Whether you attend local events, travel to regional meets, or read through its bi-monthly publications, the "NAWCC Bulletin" and the "Mart," your horological world will be enhanced immeasurably. The NAWCC also has The National Watch & Clock Museum and a library and research center.

At one local NAWCC meeting I attended in San Leandro, California, years ago, I was standing by my table at what they call the "mart." A fellow behind me walked up to his own table and unceremoniously upended a grocery bag full of old watches. Being a watchmaker, I cringed at seeing all those vintage watches being banged together as he poured them out. Suddenly, here was this huge pile of old wrist and pocket watches laying there. This, of course, is an urban prospector's dream come true. I am sure he did this to get everybody's attention, because in 30 seconds, he was swamped with treasure hunters. I just turned around and started pawing through the pile. One of the watches I picked up was an old mid-sized nickel silver pocket watch. It was Swiss, but had no name on the dial. I noticed that the hinged back could be opened easily, so I quickly did so. Inside I noticed the "flying hourglass" insignia of a Longines. I also noticed that the balance wobbled—a sure sign of a broken balance staff. I snapped it shut, held the watch up and asked the guy how much he wanted. He glanced at it and said $10. But when I pointed out it had a broken staff and asked if he would take $7.50, he said OK.

Three months later, I entered the description and serial number of this watch into a worldwide contest the Longines Watch Company was conducting. The company was searching for the 100 oldest Longines watches in the world. Grand prize was a free trip to its factory in Switzerland, where the winner would be presented with a gold watch. My little watch didn't win the grand prize, but it turned out to be number 87 out of the top 100. Longines sent me a large and very beautiful hardbound book filled with the colorful history of its company. The book is one of those $200 coffee-table types, which I will enjoy for the rest of my life. Not bad for a little $7.50 watch discovered at a NAWCC mart (see photo on P. 20).

Another regional meet that my wife Kristy and I spent a few days at stands out in my mind. It was held in Reno, Nevada, inside a huge casino hotel complex. I remember taking a break from all the excitement of the meet and walking out of the NAWCC mart room and directly into a casino area there. I was with three fellow watch buddies and as the four of us walked down the aisle of this plush, colorful, high-energy casino, I stopped and started to laugh. "OK you guys," I said, "Everybody look down at your wrists." We all stopped and looked down. All four of us were wearing two watches—one on each wrist! The true watch lovers that we were, we had each bought a special vintage watch at the meet and had strapped it on to check its accuracy and to enjoy our finds. Off we all walked through the crowded casino, two-fisted urban prospectors each wearing two watches and enjoying every minute of it.

This contest-winning Longines, circa 1878, was found at an NAWCC mart.

American Watchmakers-Clockmakers Institute

The American Watchmakers-Clockmakers Institute (AWI), located in Harrison, Ohio, is a not-for-profit trade association for watchmakers and clockmakers. AWI is dedicated to the advancement of its members and their professions through educational and technical services. You do not have to be a watchmaker to join the AWI. It is a great association for those interested in the restoration aspect of watch collecting. The AWI has a very informative monthly publication, "The Horological Times," which contains features written by recognized experts dealing with the techniques of servicing and repairing watches, clocks, and the functional characteristics of mechanical, electronic, and antique timepieces. This, combined with a large classified ad section and regular watch industry news, provides a great resource for all horologists. The AWI also has a movement bank/material search network. The American Watchmakers-Clockmakers Institute is the place to start for anyone who is considering becoming a watchmaker or repair person. They have an Academy of Watchmaking, bench courses, and a certification program.

The AWI Mission Statement is: "The American Watchmakers-Clockmakers Institute is the premier international organization dedicated to preserving and promoting the highest standards of workmanship in the horological crafts. It is the role of AWI to set the standard of excellence to be applied to the quality of instruction for both the restoration and repair practices that are taught worldwide."

I am a member of AWI and I highly recommend the association. It is the perfect source for locating watchmakers in your area and tracking down parts and information. The AWI has an educational library and a museum. You can visit its great Web site, too, at www.awi-net.org.

MEMBER

American Watchmakers-Clockmakers Institute
701 Enterprise Drive   Harrison, OH 45030
http://www.awi-net.org

Member decal for the American Watchmakers-Clockmakers Institute.

A Longines ad from the early 1900s.

Condition, Condition, Condition

Chapter III

At some point after you have made the decision to become an urban prospector and search for watch treasure, you will need to acquire a few basic "tools of the trade."

When I'm out urban prospecting, I always carry my small "watch inspection kit" in a belt pouch that contains the following items: One good pair of tweezers, one rubber vacuum case opener for pocket watch (screw back) cases, one watchcase opening knife (for wrist and pocket watches), one decent loupe for magnification, and a few small plastic Zip-lock bags to place the timepieces I find in. Armed with these few tools, a person can inspect most pre-1960 timepieces.

Now you are ready to check out your very first stash of newly acquired watches from friends and family you have spread out all over the kitchen table. Get a feel for handling them, holding them, and inspecting their tops and bottoms, sides and ends. At this point, you can start to develop your "extra sensory perception" while attempting to understand what this little machine went through while strapped on the wrist of, or bounced around in the pocket of, its previous owner. Use all of your senses—this will come in handy when out in the field—and look at the overall condition of the watch. Did its owner take good care of it? Was it abused, thrashed, crashed, scratched, and dropped? Is it ticking? Is it tocking? Is it humming? Is it silent? Does it rattle? Does it have apparent moisture inside the crystal? All of this early experience will come in handy when you go out into the "real" world and begin your urban prospecting. Go ahead and start grading them on a scale of 1 to 10 (10 being the highest). This is good practice for when you are out in the field, since you will need to access the condition of timepieces quickly, and occasionally not under the best circumstances—inadequate lighting, minimal tools available for inspection, time constraints, etc. After checking out as many watches as you have on hand at home, you will be ready to go out buying in the field.

It has been said that the three most important things to consider when buying, selling, or appraising real estate are "location, location, location." Well, where vintage watches are concerned, you can say "condition, condition, condition" as being the most important considerations. When you are contemplating buying a watch, you must ask yourself over and over, "What is the true state that this timepiece is in, at present?" You must study the watch closely and ascertain its accurate condition. Is it in average condition? Is it in mint condition? How do I tell?

Visualize the following scenario: Jim Dandy is given a Waltham pocket watch for Christmas in 1908. Jim's cousin, Dicky Birdeye, bought it for him at a fine jewelry store in the city. The jeweler bought it fresh, in the box, from the manufacturer and placed it on a shelf underneath his showcase. The watch was not set out as a showroom model, was not handled, nor did it receive any "shop wear." In fact, the only time the lid to the box was opened was by the jeweler when he got it and then, again, when he showed it to the customer, Jim's relative. Once again it was opened, after Jim had unwrapped it from under the Christmas tree. It just so happened that Jim Dandy had been given another cool watch earlier that year at his retirement party, and so he thanked his cousin Dicky for the gift and closed the lid forever. He liked his newfangled gold wrist watch he had been given for his retirement and wore it constantly. He didn't want to hurt Dicky's feelings by returning the gift, so he carefully placed the watch, still in the original box, under his socks in his top dresser drawer.

Twenty-one years later when his stockbroker called to let him know his portfolio had just vaporized, Jim had a massive stroke and died. Jim's wife found the watch while going through his things soon after he had passed and decided to give it to their grandson Earl. Earl's folks figured it was too nice of a watch for a 12-year-old, and told Jim's wife that they would hold on to it until Earl graduated from college and present it to him then. They carefully placed it in their top dresser drawer under the socks. Time wore on and in 1941, Earl graduated from college and was given the Waltham. He opened up the box, looked at the pocket watch, and thanked his folks profusely. The next day he received his draft notice into the army. He carefully placed the Waltham, still in the original box, in his dresser drawer under his old socks. He figured it could remain there safely until his return. Four years went by and Earl came back from the war. He married his high school sweetheart and proceeded to do his next patriotic duty.

In the following years, Earl had six children, all girls. Earl never did carry a pocket watch, but really liked the old Tavannes wrist watch his wife had given him and wore it for 10 years until it quit working. He parked it next to the old Waltham, in the top drawer of his oak dresser, under the socks where it had laid for years. Earl didn't want to use the pocket watch because it still looked as good as new and he was afraid that if he wore it, he might damage it. In fact, Earl spent the next 45 years wearing Timex wrist watches. One day Earl got a call from his stockbroker who informed him that his high tech stock portfolio had vaporized. Earl went into brain fog shock at the news, contracted terminal disinterest, and passed on a few weeks later. None of the six daughters wanted the Waltham, as they thought it was just too old and their dad never even wore it anyway. Earl's wife had a garage sale the next spring, and when asked by a young man if she had any old watches, remembered the Waltham. She decided to sell the watch right there and then.

Earl's wife went into the bedroom, opened her top dresser drawer, and retrieved the vintage Waltham. She returned to the garage and showed it to the young man. He opened the box and found an open faced, 16 Size, 23 Jewel, Waltham Vanguard pocket watch, with up and down wind indicator, in a white gold filled case. His heart raced as he looked at the pristine condition original box, and then at the Waltham Factory papers that came with the watch. Priscilla told the young man that she doubted that the old watch still worked, after all it had sat in an old sock drawer for decades. They both watched as the young man wound the Waltham up. Nothing happened. "The oil probably dried up in it and has become sticky. It's going to need a cleaning," said the young watch collector. "You can have it for $50," Priscilla said to him. "I know these old pocket watches sell for a lot more at antiques shops, but as this one doesn't run, I'll let you have it for less." The young man tried to keep his hands from trembling as he counted out the $50 Priscilla had asked for.

Visual and Mechanical Condition

In the above scenario, you can understand how a vintage watch might come out of the past, into your possession, and still be in "mint" condition. However, most watches are found in "average" condition, because the people who previously owned them wore them in their daily lives. How the person wearing it treated the watch, and what kind of regular maintenance, if any, the timepiece received, plays a big part in the overall condition of the vintage watch.

When you examine a watch, look at the dial (the face), and get a feel for what the watch has been through. Ask questions from the owner and try to learn the history of the piece. Let the watch "speak to you." A fellow watch fanatic, collector, dealer, buyer, seller, friend of mine, once said to me when I showed him one I had for sale, "The watch just doesn't speak to me." He is so very right in thinking this way. You need to reach out with your sixth sense sometimes when contemplating buying a watch and get the feel of it. This is especially true if you're going to be bidding on one, or you need to make a quick decision when in a buying situation. Or, when you are on "the excitement plan" with your credit card in hand, eyes glazed over with anticipation, and your heart is beating way over 9,000 rpm! Remember, it is *very* easy to buy a watch, but sometimes it can be *very* hard to resell it, especially if you bought high (high price and high on the idea of owning it), or didn't eyeball it closely.

What does the dial say? If your sixth sense is foggy, then tune up your other five senses to examine the watch. Is the dial an original one? This is of utmost importance to collectors, for in the past it was a common practice for watchmakers to send the dial off to be refinished, if it had even a little wear, when the watch came in for a service. The watchmaker made a little extra money and the customer now had a watch that looked brand new when they came to pick it up. If it's a Swiss watch, does it say "Switzerland," "Swiss," or "Swiss Made" on the very bottom of the dial? Does the dial have any stains, discoloration, cracks, chips, scratches, dings, or dents? Is the paint faded or partly missing? If the dial is enamel, does it have any hairline cracks that can be seen with the naked eye or under magnification? If the dial has been restored in the past and is not the original, how does the refinish work look? Was it a quality refinish job? Is it crisp? Lines straight and wording correct?

Before: Gruen, circa 1960s, in as-found condition, with a broken crystal and dirty case.

After: Gruen, Precision-auto wind, circa 1960s, after crystal replacement and case cleaned.

A 1940s' Swiss-made Gubelin in as-found condition.

A 1940s' Gubelin with crystal removed.

Gubelin, circa 1940s, refinished/restored, stainless steel, dial refinished but hands kept in original condition.

pulled out smartly, or slip back in (broken setting bridge)? Now turn the crown for setting the hands and notice how it feels. Is it hard to turn the crown or does it turn too freely (too tight or too loose cannon pinion)? Do the hands line up correctly? Do the hands hit the dial or touch the roof of the crystal? What condition is the crystal in? Is it plastic or glass? Tap it on your front teeth. With practice, you can tell the difference between the two. Plastic crystals can usually have their scratches all polished out. Glass ones are harder to restore when all scratched and chipped. Any cracks or breaks in the crystal will allow moisture and dust inside the dial area, and will need to be replaced.

Next, check out the case. Does it look original to the movement? What material is it made from? Solid gold, gold filled, gold plated, platinum, silver, nickel silver, stainless steel, chrome plated base metal? Visually, what condition is it in? Note any wear through the plating, or brass showing through; notice any dents, dings, scratches, pitting, bent, or misshapen areas. If it is a pocket watch with a threaded back and bezel, are they cross-threaded or do they screw on and off smoothly? If the case has a snap fit bezel and back, check for scratches and marring that an errant case opener knife left. If it is a hunter case pocket watch, check to see if the bezel is in place and is the correct one. If you are examining a wrist watch case, look to see if the fits are close between the body and bezel, and the back and body. Check to see if the lugs are straight.

If it is a runner, listen to the movement. Does it sound strong and steady no matter what position you hold it in? Is the movement loose inside the case—does it rattle? If it is an automatic winding-type watch, can you hear the rotor when it spins around? Is it a smooth sound or can you hear the rotor hitting the case back or the movement plate? If the watch is a complicated one, have the owner show you the different functions and how they work. Ask the seller if it is OK to open the back up and visibly check out the movement if possible. If you are able to get that far into the watch, look on the underside of the case back for screw head marks where movement case screws may have backed out and worn into the case. Also look under the case back for watchmaker marks, as they can tell you a story of how often the movement was serviced through the years.

Inspect the condition of the movement and look for rust spots, especially on the hairspring. Examine the balance wheel area. Does the balance wheel turn freely and smoothly? Does it wobble? Look closely at the screw heads holding the movement together. Look at the slots in the screw heads where the screw driver blade fits. Are they all in good shape, or have they been marked up by being removed and replaced too many times by careless repair people? There are a lot of "hackers" out in the watch world, who, after reading a couple of repair manuals and looking at a few pictures, believe that they are master watchmakers. I have opened many a fine watch to sadly see screwdriver skid marks across a bridge or plate, and screw heads broken and messed up.

Move next to the hands. Are they straight? Do the hands match and are they original? Look at the very center where the hands attach. Is it all scratched up in the center of the hands? Do they look like they have been taken off and put back on 50 times? Examine the crown. Does it look to be an original one, or does it have the watch manufacturer's logo or name on it? Does it sit up against the body of the case straight and close? Does it wobble out of round when you turn it (bent stem or crown tube)? Turn the crown. What does it feel like? Is it a smooth winding feel? When winding the mainspring does it skip or feel scratchy (winding mechanism wheels or pinion teeth problems)? Do you wind and wind and wind but never seem to get it fully wound (mainspring broken or slipping)? Pull the crown out into the setting position. Does it stay

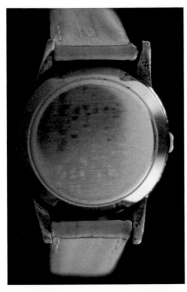

This is an example of a watch with worn lugs. Notice how the brass shows through on the back.

A "hacker" attempt at watch repair ruined this fine old Howard. Note the upper right-hand corner.

Many watch collectors are only interested in the outward appearance of their vintage watch. Whether it functions properly mechanically or not is a secondary consideration. I must say that the condition of the outward appearance is probably the most important factor in most peoples' minds, but you should get in the habit of grading the watch as a whole. Just like a cool old restored car is an eye-catcher, so, too, can a vintage watch be. But, if your neat old car doesn't run very well or doesn't have its original engine or dashboard, it reduces the value that can be placed on it. If you have not yet established a relationship with a qualified watch repair person, then seek one out as soon as possible. Just like the best doctors, they very quickly get too many clients, and it becomes a problem getting on their waiting list. Once you have found a competent watchmaker to work with, he or she will assist

you in keeping your vintage watches in top condition. Contact the American Watchmakers-Clockmakers Institute for help in finding a watchmaker in your area.

Condition, condition, condition. Always keep these words in mind when grading a watch. The closer the watch is to its original condition, the better. In our little story about Jim Dandy, his watch was in mint condition and remained so as it spent years hidden under old socks. Watches like this are rare, but can still be found. I know, because I've seen dozens of them. You will hear the term "new old stock" (NOS). These are watches that have never been sold to, or used by, anyone. These are items that perhaps an old jewelry store owner stuck in the back storage room and forgot about. Items that were last year's style (50 years ago) didn't sell, or were overstocked and put in the back of the storage cabinet at the local drug store. These are watches that are still in their original factory display boxes and still might even have the original price tags, warranty/guarantee paperwork, etc., with them.

The next best find would be a watch that was purchased and hardly ever used, like in our scenario. This would be a mint or near mint piece. Perhaps, like Jim Dandy, someone got a watch for Christmas, didn't particularly like it, and stuck it away for 37 years. Or, it might be a presentation watch, engraved and given to them at their retirement, or some special occasion, and they never wore it. Whatever the reason the person never wore the watch, bless their hearts, for this is the only way they come to be in mint condition. Remember that mint condition to one person might not be so mint to another. This term gets thrown around quite a bit, and you really must get down to the nitty gritty with it. When buying a watch, you can use the rating scale on P. 26 to help place a value on the timepiece.

Some watches just need a good surface cleaning and polishing, as this 1950's Elgin found in good running condition.

10	Positively mint	NOS, unused, factory fresh, and still in the original box.
9	Mint +	Pristine, in original box, perhaps slightly or rarely used, but looks as if it was never used.
8	Mint	In original condition with only very little use and no scratches, marks, or wear.
7	Near mint	In original condition and used, but with only faint marks or wear.
6	Fine +	Taken very good care of, with original parts used in any repairs or restoration. Very little scratches, marks, or wear.
5	Fine	Very crisp with only minor wear, marks, and scratches. Still has original case, dial may have had quality restoration done, has original movement.
4	Average	Wear from normal use for its age, but still with original case, dial (may have been refinished), and movement. Normal dings, wear marks, and scratches expected from daily use.
3	Fair	Well used, and may not have the original case, dial, or movement.
2	Poor	Broken, not working, parts missing, very well worn, but restorable.
1	Junk	Totally worn out, damaged, rust, parts watch only.

Restoration

When you find a vintage watch worthy of restoration, you must consider all of what that entails. Let us say that you discover a wrist watch in 4 grade (average) condition, with a badly discolored dial. To restore the dial or *not* to restore the dial, *that* is the question.

Generally speaking, a dial has to be fairly well gone before I refinish it. Collectors always prefer a watch with an original dial. However, if it is just plain ugly, then get it refinished. Sometimes it is a tough call and a lot of the decision rests with what you plan to do with the watch after restoration. If you enjoy the look of the watch and plan to wear it, then getting the dial redone is a question of personal preference. If you obtained the watch with the desire to resell it, then you might consider cleaning up the case, crystal, and movement, but leave the decision to restore the dial to the next owner. However, if the dial is too ugly, there might not be a next owner anytime soon.

The "before and after" photographs included in these pages will give you an idea of when I decided to send the dial in for restoration. I have, in the past, attempted to clean painted metal watch dials that were just soiled looking. Ninety percent of the time when I tried this, however, the paint just started coming off. You must be careful and examine the dial closely to see if it will stand up to a light cleaning. Your watchmaker will know best what to recommend as far as dial cleaning goes. Usually you're better off not trying to clean it. Enamel dials are easier to have cleaned, as the enamel has been kiln fired onto metal

A 1930's Bulova with badly rusted hands and dial.

The same 1930's Bulova, with dial restored and hands replaced.

and the lettering and numbers are more stable. Repairs can also be made on enamel dials (see photo examples), but keep in mind that enamel is like glass and you must be careful with them. Hairline cracks can grow and chunks can fall off if these dials are mistreated. A huge percent of vintage wrist and pocket watches with enamel dials have pronounced or faint hairline cracks in them. It is exciting to find one of these fine old watches with a perfect dial on it. Enamel dials with hairlines can be placed in an "ultrasonic cleaner" and the hairlines will disappear. However, they will return as soon as dust and dirt starts settling in the cracks again. Examine them closely with a good loupe to determine if they are free of hairlines or not.

Many times, a watch just needs a good polish and a new crystal to look new again. To restore vintage watchcases, there are watchcase repair experts that can re-plate gold-plated cases, repair broken hinges, make new bezels, fix holes, dings, and deep scratches. Solid gold cases are easier to polish up and restore than gold plated or gold-filled ones. Gold-filled cases are the next best thing to solid gold (gold filled is like an Oreo cookie lying on its side, there is basc metal inside, usually brass, with thick plates of gold on the outsides). In the past, pocket watchcases were sometimes marked "5 Years," "10 Years," "Warranted 20 Years," etc. This is an indication of how thick the gold plates were when the case was made. Can you imagine anything warranted for 20 years nowadays? It's amazing that these gold-filled cases were made so well that the manufacturer could guarantee they would hold up for 10 or 20 years. Actually, most of these vintage gold-filled cases lasted many times longer than their warranty before any of the gold wore off to reveal the brass sandwiched inside. Rolled gold plate, sometimes stamped on cases as R.G.P., is the same as gold-fill, except the gold plating is thinner than gold-filled cases. The R.G.P. watchcases did not hold up as long as the gold filled ones, but would last better than the next category, which is the gold-electroplated case. These cases just have a few microns of gold plating. Great care has to be used when polishing and restoring them to original finish.

A 1920s' Gelbros, with broken crystal.

The same Gelbros Swiss, circa 1920s, with fancy engraved case, radium hands, and glass crystal replaced.

Restoration of gold filled and rolled gold-plated cases is tricky business. On wrist watch cases, the sharp edges usually wear through first—the corners, high spots, edges of the bezel and back, under the lugs, and also the tips of the lugs are the first to go. The case repairer must solder and/or re-plate the case. Depending on the severity of the wear, many times it just isn't worth the time and money to fully restore a badly worn-through gold-filled or R.G.P. case.

A damaged 1890's enamel pocket watch dial.

The same enamel pocket watch dial, after the author repaired the damaged areas.

Restoring the movement of a vintage watch depends on the age of the timepiece and availability of parts. If the movement just needs a cleaning and oiling, this is to be considered standard maintenance. If the movement has broken or rusted parts, you will need an estimate for repair and restoration from a competent watchmaker or repair person. Watches manufactured prior to the 1950s might not be shock protected (see photos) and must be examined for balance staff problems. If it was manufactured prior to the 1940s, it definitely wasn't shock protected, since very few watches had this feature prior to that time. When a watch is dropped or shocked severely, the balance staff and the crystal are the first to break. When examining a watch, see

that the balance turns while the watch is held in various positions. A watch with a broken balance staff may work in one position, but not in another. A watch that is very old, or one that is very rare where only a few were originally made or have survived, can usually have parts made for it if none are available. This is most always an expensive and time-consuming process.

I could go on and on about watch repair and restoration, but suffice it to say that the more you inspect and handle these little machines, the better you will become at knowing what to look for, and the better you will become at judging their true condition, condition, condition.

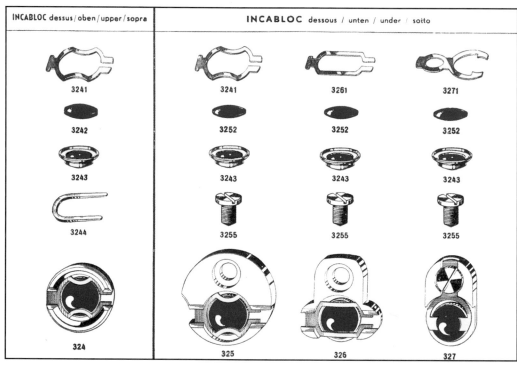

Samples of Incabloc shock absorber systems.

A 1950's Bulova with a badly discolored dial.

The restored Bulova, circa 1950s, gold filled, diamond dial, after dial restoration.

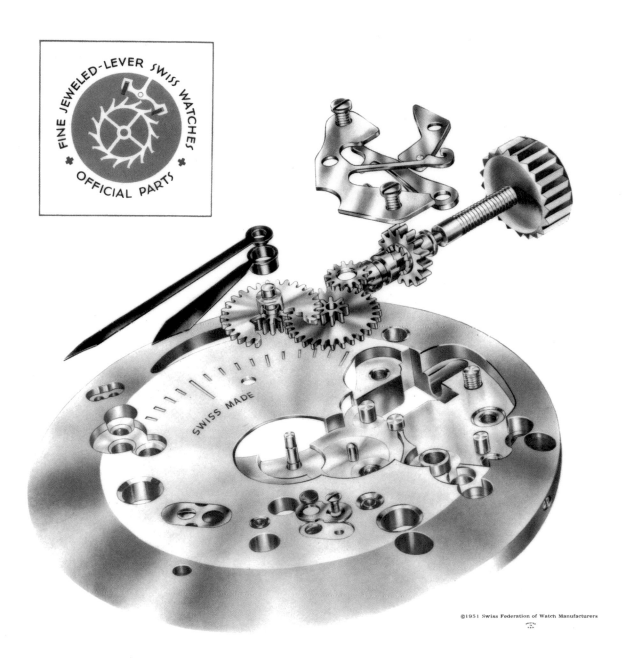

FINE JEWELED-LEVER SWISS WATCHES · OFFICIAL PARTS

SWISS MADE

©1951 Swiss Federation of Watch Manufacturers

COLOR ILLUSTRATION
SCALED 10 TO 1

Official Swiss Parts Identification

NO.	NOMENCLATURE	NO.	NOMENCLATURE
100	Plate	**410**	Winding pinion
240	Cannon-pinion (steel)	**435**	Yoke (clutch lever)
260	Minute wheel	**440**	Yoke spring
333	Cap jewel 8 shaped	**443**	Setting lever (detent)
401	Stem	**445**	Setting lever spring
407	Clutch wheel	**450**	Setting wheel

The WATCHMAKERS OF SWITZERLAND

SWISS FEDERATION WATCH MANUFACTURERS

Under the dial of a Swiss wrist watch, view of setting mechanism.

Buying

and

Selling

First, let me warn you right now of the problem of fakes in the market. Most of us have seen the cheap fake Rolex watches that are out there by the millions. If you are not sure how a fake Rolex measures up to the real McCoy, go to your local Rolex dealer and ask to see a few.

Fake Rolexes hurt dealers' businesses and I'm sure they wouldn't mind letting you handle a couple. That way, you can get the feel and heft, and notice the craftsmanship and attention to detail that goes into making each one. Newer fakes are easy to spot once you have spent the time checking out the real thing.

An example of an early cylinder-type escapement.

A metal toy truck, with Longines Watch Co. advertisement.

However, now that I've said that, a friend of mine, in his travels, came across a fake made to look exactly like a 1940s vintage Rolex. These are very hard for the rookie to identify and you must be careful. Always buy from a reputable dealer and remember to pay attention to detail and workmanship when inspecting the piece. There are some really good fakes of Omega watches out there and I myself was nearly fooled by one until I removed the back to inspect the movement. The outside of the watch, including the dial, looked very authentic and the finish was relatively crisp. Once I peeked in the back, though, I knew it was fake. Be careful you don't get stung.

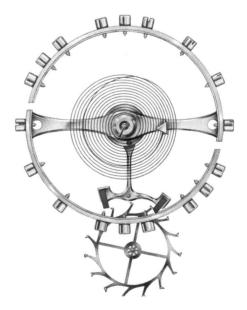

An example of modern lever escapement.

An example of Swiss chronograph movement.

Buying

If you are just starting to collect vintage watches, it is a good idea to concentrate on just one kind of watch: American 21-jewel pocket watches or automatic-wind wrist watches, or just one brand/maker of watches, such as Hamilton, Waltham, Longines, Omega, Gruen, Mido, Vacheron Constantin, etc. This way, you can become fairly knowledgeable about your particular favorite watches in a relatively short amount of time. In my early collecting days, I would buy anything and everything as long as I thought I was getting a deal. After ending up with drawers full of every kind of watch, in every kind of condition (mostly broken), I decided to be a little pickier. If you run into good deals on watches that are not the kind you collect, you can always use them for "trading stock" to other dealers or watchmakers, who are always looking for parts. Just be careful not to buy everything you come across or you can spend a lot of money and not have as much to show for it. It is a far better investment to buy a couple mint or near mint timepieces than to buy two dozen below-average-condition clunkers.

When you have discovered a watch you desire to possess, you must truthfully ask yourself a few questions. How you answer these questions will help you decide how much you're willing to spend on any given watch. What are you buying the watch for? Are you going to keep it and add the piece to your collection? Are you going to resell the watch? If you are going to sell it, are you going to sell it at a wholesale price or a retail price?

When you ask the seller how much they want for the watch and they say, "I was hoping you could tell me what it is worth," you will have to do some quick calculations in your head. If you are going to keep the watch for your own collection, you can pay a little more for it, as you don't have to think about turning a profit. If you plan to resell it, it is good to remember to "buy low and sell high." Until I really studied the market, I used to "buy high and sell low." Then I discovered it was more fun the other way. Knowledge is the key.

When you are speaking to someone on the phone about a watch and, after finding out what kind it is (gent's, lady's) and who the maker is, here are some questions to ask:

1. Does the watch wind up and does it run? Can you pull the crown (winder) out and set the hands?

2. What color is the dial (face) and what condition is it in? Is it the original dial or has it been restored/refinished at some point in the past? What is written (printed) on the dial? If it is a Swiss watch, it should have "Swiss," "Swiss Made," or "Switzerland" printed at the very bottom of the dial, below the six o'clock position.

3. What material is the case made of—stainless steel, yellow gold, white gold, gold filled, rolled gold plate, gold electroplate, silver, nickel, chrome plate?

4. What condition is the case in? Any dents? Dings? Scratches? Worn spots? Is there any engraving on the watch?

5. What is the history of the piece?

6. How would the overall condition and appearance of the watch be rated? Average? Fine? Mint?

7. What is the asking price?

You will soon get a feel for the person you are talking to, and for the watch they're selling. Listen very closely and try to picture the piece in your mind as they describe it to you.

The following are a few tips for making an offer on a vintage watch. This part of the process can be an art in itself. You can get people mad at you, embarrass yourself to no end, and help create some bad vibes if you don't proceed with caution. If you are at an auction or an antiques shop where the price is already fixed, you cannot expect to do much bargaining. However, if you are buying over the phone from an ad you placed, or at a flea market, garage sale, or estate sale, you might be able to negotiate the price. If I ask the seller how much they want for the watch and they say they don't know and ask me what it's worth, I tell them exactly what I know to be true.

Let's say, for instance, it is a circa early 1960s stainless steel Omega "Seamaster" automatic-wind wrist watch that needs servicing, as it has sat in a drawer for 20 years. You have judged the watch to be in the #6, Fine + condition. In this scenario, we will say that the watch is working OK and doesn't need any parts; it just needs a cleaning, oiling, and polishing. In this case, I will tell them their watch, when serviced and in excellent running condition, is worth around $295 to a collector. But I also tell them I have to put some time, effort, and money into the piece to bring it up to standard, and then will have to search out a collector who loves the watch enough to part with $295 for it. Since we also live in good old capitalist America, I also note I need to make a little profit for my efforts and can therefore offer them $125 for their watch. After I explain this to the person—and especially people from an older generation—nine times out of 10 they say they understand I've got to make a little something on the deal and my offer sounds like a fair price.

Whenever they don't know what a watch is worth and ask me how much I will give them for it, or that they were hoping I would tell them what it's worth, I immediately go for the honest truth. People appreciate it when you look them in the eye and tell them exactly as it is. They will tell their friends, too, and you will get referrals by being upfront, discreet, and honest. Of course, you will have to do some studying and know your approximate values when you do this and you must study the market to know what's hot and what's not. Now then, it would be a really super good deal if you found this same watch at an antiques collective or flea market, with a price tag of $59.95 on it. That can happen, too.

What to buy?

So, what's hot? Well, beauty is in the eye of the beholder, of course, and different strokes for different folks and such, but generally, as for wrist watches, I believe you can never go wrong by picking up good quality stainless steel men's pieces, especially brand name automatic-wind wrist watches. Unusually shaped wrist watches, watches with complications (day, date, chronograph functions, moonphase, alarm, world time, repeater, etc.), limited edition pieces (watches the factory didn't make many of), early wrist watches from the 1910s and 1920s, and rose gold (pink gold) wrist watches are your best bets. Stainless steel wrist watches from the 1940s through the 1960s seem to be real hot collectibles. As for pocket watches, look for early examples of the top American and Swiss makers (low serial numbers), American railroad grade and railroad approved 16- and 18-size pocket watches, hunter case watches, pocket watches with multicolored dials, and high-grade Swiss pocket watches, especially ones made in the 1960s and 1970s, which are rather hard to find.

As for ladies' watches, what is highly collectible seems to be wide open for debate. At present, tiny ladies' watches from the 1940s through the 1960s do not seem to be highly sought after. I wish I had a nickel for every one of these little machines I've run across. It seems that the women in America all need glasses and can't read the time on them or something—I certainly need my glasses to see them! With women's liberation of the last half of the 20th century, it seems that the larger watches have become more popular with ladies. Higher grade, name brand, women's wrist watches such as Movado, Longines, Omega, Rolex, Cartier, Vacheron Constantin, etc. are always popular no matter what size, especially if they are unusual in some way or have diamonds or other stones set into their cases. I like early (larger pieces) 1910s or 1920s Elgin, Hamilton, and Gruen ladies' watches, especially if they have enamel on them. But the itty bitty little granny-type watches—Bulova, Gruen, Waltham, Hamilton, Elgin, Swiss, etc.—of which they made bazillions of, do not seem to be real popular at this time. I have heard that as the Chinese economy expands, the men there will be buying these little retro wrist watches for their women friends. That could be a huge market if one could figure out how to supply it.

Ladies' pocket watches and pendant watches are a bit fragile and rather high-maintenance items, if you are going to bounce them around in everyday use. For this reason, I don't see a huge interest in this area. Still, the enamel ladies' pieces are little works of art and are sought after for their beauty. The whole area of collectible ladies' watches is a huge market waiting to catch fire. It seems that men are the biggest collectors of watches and have been for some time. I would love to see more women get excited about collecting the smaller timepieces, as they are truly marvels of miniature engineering, craftsmanship, and beauty. The watch factories across the world have, since they began mass production, employed thousands of women to assemble the watches. It is high time the ladies started buying back, and collecting, what they themselves helped to create.

Selling

OK, urban prospector, so you want to sell a watch, huh? The following are some points to consider. Are you going to guarantee the watch or are you going to use the old flea-market rule of "20 seconds or 20 feet?" In other words, you'll only guarantee the piece for 20 seconds after the buyer purchases it or until the buyer gets 20 feet away from you with it; after that, they're on their own. If you use this rule, you will need to inform potential buyers that perhaps the watch has been lying in an old drawer for 42 years and, although it might tick for a bit, it isn't going to tock and you are not guaranteeing it to keep good time. Inform the buyer they should consider having it serviced should they want to wear it; or, in the case of pocket watches, carry it. If you have spent time and money going through the watch and have it all polished and running great, let the buyer know this also. Explain to them all that was done to the timepiece—overhaul, services, parts replaced, etc. If you have had the watch fully serviced and can now guarantee it to run and keep time, the selling price should reflect this. Some collectors would rather take care of the servicing on their own (they do it themselves or take it to their trusted watchmaker), as this is part of their excitement and collecting fun.

Where do you go to sell your watch?

As a rule, collectors pay the highest prices for watches. They are going to keep the watches they purchase and don't have to worry so much about saving room for profit when buying them. Watch dealers, of course, need to buy low and sell high to stay in business; therefore, you won't generally get as much for your watches from them. However, you might sit on your watch for a long, long time waiting to find the right collector to come by and fall in love with it. Dealers are in touch with many collectors and you might be able to turn your watches over faster through them.

To sell watches, you need to go where the dealers and collectors go; the Internet, AWI, NAWCC, antiques shops, antiques shows, auction houses, networking, advertising, etc. You can rent a space in an antiques collective to display and sell your timepieces. Most of these collectives rent space in their showcases and are perfect spots for selling small items like watches. You can also offer your items to dealers who already have showcase spots set up with watches. Joining the AWI and the NAWCC, and attending local and regional meets are excellent avenues for selling watches. Plus, it's a lot of fun.

The Internet (my favorite spot is eBay) is a great avenue for selling your watches, since you are placing them in front of hundreds and maybe even thousands of watch lovers and potential buyers. You can join an online auction service and in no time at all conduct your very own watch auctions. There are also many Web sites set up by vintage watch dealers and you can contact them directly about selling your timepieces, as they are always looking to acquire more items for their businesses. Many times these dealers are also into the watch repair business, and so you can offer them watches that are not running or that need restoration. You can list your watches online with big auction houses such as Southeby's, if you don't mind paying them a percentage of the sale. If you want to display and sell watches from your collection, you can look into setting up your very own vintage watch Web site. There are Web-based "chat rooms" for sharing information, too. The only downside to the Internet is that it can sometimes lack the "human touch." One of my greatest pleasures is to hang out with other watch fans and yak for hours on the subject, while showing our watches, sharing buying tips, swapping selling stories, and sharing watch knowledge.

I have successfully sold hundreds and hundreds of watches over the years through NAWCC, setting up spots in collectives, and on the Internet. Wherever you go to sell your watches, remember this: Always describe the watch very accurately and truthfully. Don't sell any hidden surprises to people. If you don't know everything about a piece, then tell prospective buyers that. Point out any known flaws so the buyer knows exactly what they're buying. The golden rule applies here. The reward in doing this is obvious—people appreciate the honesty and they will become repeat customers.

Watch Values and Identification

Chapter V

"What is this watch that I just inherited from Uncle Harry really worth?" you may ask yourself. If you think you have a valuable vintage watch in your possession and want to know its value, then you must gather knowledge about it. This book is meant to be a guide for you in the search for answers to the question of "What is the current market value of my watch?" The key word here is "guide." That is what this book is meant to be. This guide is not the last word on the value of watches, and it is not meant to be the complete "watch bible and encyclopedia" on the subject. I have endeavored to give you, the reader, a snapshot slice of the world of watches.

As Rene Rondeau says in his book, *Hamilton Wristwatches: A Collector's Guide*, "Watch prices are at best a moving target." The values of vintage watches change with trends in the market, the state of our economy, tastes in personal attire, what era in time happens to be cool and trendy this season, etc. All I do know is that values of vintage watches have done nothing but go up and up in the past two decades, and I don't see it slowing down.

The watch prices listed in this guide are for watches in good running condition, with all parts in place, band and crystal, etc. The prices listed are for the most part *retail* prices. They are prices that one would expect to pay in a retail environment like an antiques shop, vintage/estate jewelry establishment, professional watch dealer, or fine auction house. I have listed price ranges of watches in *average* to *near mint* condition. If your watch is in need of repairs or is in less than average condition, the value of the timepiece will be less than the average price, to reflect some of the cost of repairs and restoration. If the watch in question is in *mint* condition, then the sky is the limit and you can name your price. The limiting factors are condition, rarity, and demand.

To give you an example of how much of a moving target watch prices can be, I will relate a story that a watch dealer friend of mine told me. This friend rents a spot in a

large antiques collective in one town, owns a nice estate jewelry/watch shop in another town, and also operates an upscale estate jewelry shop in yet a third town. He placed a vintage watch for sale in the antiques collective. He priced it at $200, which is what, in his experience, was a good retail price. The watch sat for months and months with no activity, so he reduced the price to $150—still no activity. So, he took the watch out of the antiques store, placed it in his estate jewelry/watch shop, and put a price of $295 on it. There it sat for another long period of time with no activity or interested buyer. He then took the watch to his third location, the upscale estate jewelry shop, where he changed the price tag on it to $695. The watch sold in two weeks! What do you suppose he is going to ask for a similar watch if he should acquire one and put it up for sale? This is a perfect example, albeit an unusual one, of how watch prices can be moving targets.

In another example, I had a Hamilton Coronado wrist watch from the 1930s that sold for $1,000 more than I or my watch dealer friends thought that it would sell for. It was one of the more scarce and collectible of watches, and very much in demand, I learned through the experience. Some watches are worth more on the West Coast than on the East Coast. You must do research and get information from different resources to get an accurate value for a given watch. If you think a price is too high on a watch you plan to buy, ask yourself how hard would it be to find another one in this condition.

The watches listed in this guide are timepieces that have been bought or sold by collectors, watch dealers, antiques dealers, Internet traders, and auction houses. They will provide you with a good place to start for finding a value for your watches.

Here is a small list of the names of watches and watch manufacturers, to keep your prospector's eye out for: Agassiz, Alpina, Angelus, Assmann, Audemars Piguet, Ball Watch Co., Baume & Mercier, J.W. Benson, Benrus,

Blancpain, Breguet, Breitling, Bucherer, Bulova, Cartier, Chopard, Columbus Watch Co., Croton, Cyma, Dent, Ditisheim, Doxa, Ebel, Eberhard, Ekegren, Elgin, Eterna, Favre Leuba, Gallet, Geneve, Girard Perregaux, Glasshutte, Glycine, Goering, Golay, Gotham, Gruen, Gubelin, Hafis, Hamilton, Hampden, Harwood, Hebdomas, Helbros, Heuer, E. Howard & Co., E. Howard Watch Co. (Keystone), Huguenin, Illinois Watch Co., Ingersoll, E. Ingraham Co., International Watch Co., Junghans, Jules Jurgensen, Juvenia, Lancaster Watch Co., A. Lange & Sohne, Le Coultre, Lemania, Longines, Lucien Piccard, C. H. Meylan, Mido, Minerva, Montbrillant, Moser Cie., Movado, Ulysse Nardin, New England Watch Co., New Haven, New York Standard, Nivada, Non-Magnetic Watch Co., Ollendorf, Omega, Patek Philippe, Patria, Piaget, Pierce, Pulsar, Rado, Record, Roamer, Rockford Watch Co., Rolex, Roskopf, Rotary, Sandoz, Seiko, Seth Thomas, Shreve & Co., South Bend Watch Co., Tavannes, Tiffany & Co., Tissot, Trenton Watch Co., Universal, United States Watch Co., Vacheron Constantin, Vulcain, Wakmann, Waltham Watch Co. (American Waltham Watch Co.), Waterbury Watch Co., Westclox, Wittnauer, Wyler, Zenith, and Zodiac.

These are all watches I have run across at some point in my 26-year journey. There are many more names out there and too many to list. If a business, or even an individual, wanted to have their name placed on the dial of a watch, and if they placed a large enough order with the watch manufacturer, one could have anything printed on the dial. So it is that there are many, many watches to be found with jeweler's names, etc., printed on the dial. The following watches are but a sampling of the millions and millions that are out there waiting to be discovered.

Abbreviations used:

GF = Gold filled

HC = Hunter case

J = Jewel

LS = Lever set

OF = Open face

PS = Pin set

RR = Railroad

Gauge for measuring American movements (shown actual size).

Gauge for measuring Swiss movements (shown actual size).

Elgin, BW Raymond RR, circa 1924, 21J 16 size, GF, up-down indicator, $795-$1,295.

Hamilton, Ventura Electric, late 1950s, 18kt pink gold, very rare.

Pocket Watches

Many early watch manufacturers decorated their watch dials and cases with locomotives and other railroad scenes. This, however, does not denote them to be true railroad grade or railroad-approved timepieces. Railroad standards were implemented in the 1890s (see Chapter I) and had nothing to do with the decoration on the case or the dial of the watch.

Railroad timekeeper dial, London.

Railroad Special, specially adjusted dial.

Pocket watch with red numbers and train.

Pocket watch case, back engraved early train.

Early train engraved on case.

Railway timekeeper dial, Thomas Cooper London.

Gold pocket watch with train.

White dial with train, Swiss.

Railway timekeeper dial.

Railroad timekeeper dial, English.

Swiss train dial watch regulator.

Senate Express train.

Swiss watch, railroad train dial.

Swiss, 1900s nickel case engraved with Swiss cross with wings, wheel on earth. Railroad logo.

Nickel case with copper locomotive.

Chronometer train dial.

Locomotive engraved case back.

Engraving of locomotive on case back.

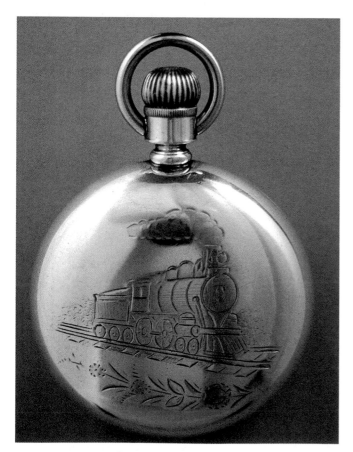

Illinois, case back train scene.

Alpina-Swiss, pocket watch packaging box, circa 1920s.

Ball Watch Co., Cleveland, Ohio

Founded in the early 1890s by Webb C. Ball. Famous for its marketing of high-grade railroad watches produced by companies such as Elgin, Hamilton, Illinois, and Waltham. The company's pocket watches are highly prized by collectors today.

Ball, 16 size official railroad standard, 21J RR, GF case, $400-$900.

Ball dial, commercial standard (Swiss), 16 size, dial only, $50-$150.

Ball 999B, circa 1900s, 21J 16 size, $695-$1,195.

Columbus Watch Co., Columbus, Ohio

Founded in 1882 and sold in 1903 to establish the South Bend Watch Co. in Indiana.

Columbus, Railway King, circa 1899, 18 size 16J Railway King movement, nickel case-Sidewinder, $300-$600.

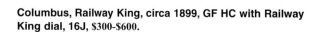

Columbus, Railway King, circa 1899, GF HC with Railway King dial, 16J, $300-$600.

Columbus movement.

Columbus, 18 size, 16J Railway King movement.

Dudley Watch Co.

Started in the early 1920s, this company of Lancaster, Pennsylvania, produced a limited number of pocket watches in which the bridges took the form of Masonic symbols.

Dudley Masonic movement, serial #5858.

Dudley Masonic, circa late 1940s, 12 size, third model, display back, YGF, $1,500-$2,500.

Elgin (Elgin National Watch Co.), Elgin, Illinois

Founded in 1864, this company produced more jeweled watches than any other in America during its more than 90-year history. The company made low-end watches, all the way up throug its famous high-quality railroad grades. These railroad pocket watches are highly sought after, as is the company's very collectible Art Deco wrist watches.

Elgin, Veritas, circa 1901, dual time zone, sterling 21J 18 size, $395-$795.

Elgin, Veritas case.

Elgin, Veritas 21 J RR movement.

Elgin, BW Raymond, circa 1908, 19J 18 size, GF case, double sunk dial, $175-$375.

Elgin/BW Raymond, 18 size 19J movement.

Elgin, circa 1879, 18 size, sweep second/doctor's watch, GF, $395-$795.

Elgin, 18 size movement, doctor's watch with sweep seconds.

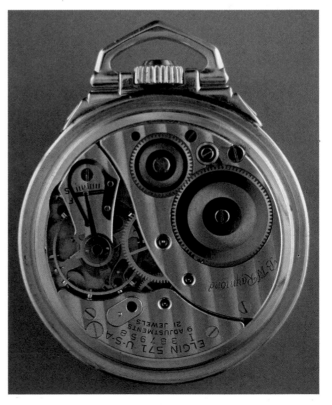

Elgin, BW Raymond RR, #571, circa 1940, 16 size, GF, 21J 9 adj., $200-$500.

Elgin, BW Raymond #571, 21J movement.

Elgin, circa 1886, 17J LS, GF box hinge case, engraved horse, $295-$595.

Elgin movement view, circa 1910, nickel display case, 17J 18 size, $95-$225.

Elgin RR, circa 1902, grade 270/three-finger bridge, 21J 16 size, nickel case, $295-$495.

Elgin, three-finger bridge movement, Grade 270.

Elgin, circa 1896, 21J 16 size, 14kt fancy HC, $595-$1,095.

Elgin, 21J, three-finger bridge, high-grade movement #156.

Elgin, BW Raymond RR, circa 1924, 21J 16 size, GF, up-down indicator, $795-$1,295.

Elgin/Montgomery dial RR, 6 size 21J, GF, incorrect bow, $225-$495.

Elgin, Father Time RR, 16 size 21J movement, $200-$475.

Elgin, circa 1919, note sub-seconds at 3:00, 15J 16 size, WGF/metal dial, $65-$175.

Elgin, 24-hour military-style dial, circa 1902, 16 size, nickel silver case, $195 -$350.

Elgin, U.S. eagle emblem on case.

Elgin, convertible movement, circa 1880, 16 size, $195-$395.

Elgin, multicolored dial, double sunk with yellow and green gold appliqué, 16 size, new-old factory stock, circa 1915, sold for $750.

The ELGIN
(B. W. RAYMOND)

has EARNED *its popularity*
with America's Railroad men

Earned it by *accuracy* . . . on-the-second accuracy . . . undeviating and unfailing. There is no more dependable watch in America. For this famous watch summarizes all that 60 years of tireless test, study and invention has taught the ELGIN experts about watch making.

[The B. W. RAYMOND . . . (illustrated here) . . . ELGIN'S deluxe Railroad Watch . . . has 21-jewel movement, 8 adjustments (5 of them to position) . . . Special-design screw case, green, white, or yellow gold filled . . . non-pull-out bow . . . new, improved dust-proof features . . . complies with all railroad systems' requirements.]

Michigan Watch Co.
DIAMONDS
WATCHES AND JEWELRY

Elgin BW Raymond ad.

Elgin, Masonic dial, circa 1920s, GF, $200-$400.

Elgin, flip-out stand, circa 1927, 17J 12 size, white gold, $494–$795.

Elgin, 17J 12 size, movement view.

ELGIN THIN MODEL WATCHES

The most popular models of the famous Elgin line. Distinguished for their style and timekeeping qualities. Appropriate, useful and acceptable gifts. All complete Elgin products; cased, timed and regulated at the factory. Attractive gift boxes. Illustrations ⅝ actual size.   *Prices Subject to Wholesale Discounts. See Page 2.*

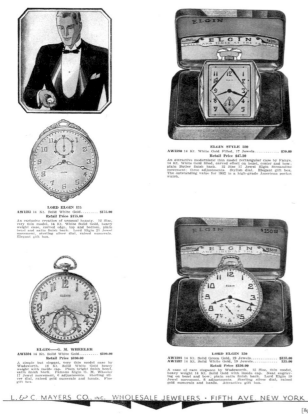

ELGIN STYLE 520
AW1590 14 Kt. White Gold Filled, 17 Jewels............. $30.00
Retail Price $47.50

An attractive modernistic thin model rectangular case by Fahys. 14 Kt. White Gold filled, carved effect on bezel, center and bow; plain Butler finish back. 12 Size 17 Jewel Elgin Streamline movement; three adjustments. Stylish dial. Elegant gift box. The outstanding value for 1932 in a high-grade American pocket watch.

LORD ELGIN 175
AW1593 14 Kt. Solid White Gold.......... $175.00
Retail Price $175.00

An exclusive creation of unusual beauty. 12 Size, very thin model, 14 Kt. Solid White Gold, heavy weight case, carved edge, top and bottom, plain bezel and satin finish back. Lord Elgin 21 Jewel movement, sterling silver dial, raised numerals. Elegant gift box.

ELGIN—G. M. WHEELER
AW1594 14 Kt. Solid White Gold.......... $100.00
Retail Price $100.00

A simple but elegant, very thin model case by Wadsworth, 14 Kt. Solid White Gold heavy weight with inside cap. Plain bright finish bezel, satin finish back. Famous Elgin G. M. Wheeler 17 Jewel movement, 6 adjustments. Sterling silver dial, raised gold numerals and hands. Fine gift box.

LORD ELGIN 150
AW1591 14 Kt. Solid Green Gold, 19 Jewels......... $155.00
AW1592 14 Kt. Solid White Gold, 19 Jewels......... $155.00
Retail Price $150.00

A case of rare elegance by Wadsworth, 12 Size, thin model, heavy weight 14 Kt. Solid Gold with inside cap. Neat engraving on bezel and bow; plain satin finish back. Lord Elgin 19 Jewel movement, 6 adjustments. Sterling silver dial, raised gold numerals and hands. Attractive gift box.

L. & C. MAYERS CO., INC. WHOLESALE JEWELERS · FIFTH AVE. NEW YORK

[89]

Elgin, 12 size, thin watches ad.

Elgin, shown free standing.

Elgin, "Dexter Street," circa 1873, 10 size, KW KS, 14kt, $295-$795.

Elgin, Dexter Street movement.

Elgin, circa 1900s, fancy enamel HC, 14kt, 6 size, case, 14kt chain with fob, floral motif with petite floral chain to floral ball, original velvet box, $2,250-$2,750.

Elgin, Dexter Street.

Elgin, circa 1886, 11J 6 size, 14kt HC, $295-$795.

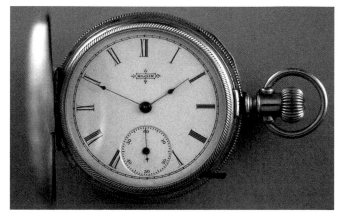

Elgin, circa 1888, 6 size, GF HC LS, $295-$595.

Elgin, 14kt engraved bird motif case.

Elgin case front.

Elgin, fancy engraved case.

Elgin case back.

Elgin, early images of children on dial, 6 size, chrome case, $95-$195.

Elgin movement.

Elgin, circa 1895, 7J 0 size, GF HC, $95-$295.

Elgin movement.

ILLUSTRATED TRADE PRICE LIST

145

ELGIN (ILLINOIS) NATIONAL WATCH COMPANY.

Movements Only. List Prices Each.

18 SIZE, STEM WIND, HUNTING, NAMED.

B. W. Raymond, Nickel, Expansion Balance, Adjusted, 15 Jewels in Settings, Patent Regulator, Breguet Hair Spring, Double Sunk Dial............................. $40 00
B. W. Raymond, Gilded, Expansion Balance, Adjusted, 15 Jewels in Settings, Patent Regulator, Breguet Hair Spring, Double Sunk Dial............................. 35 00
H. H. Taylor, Nickel, Patent Regulator, Adjusted......... 30 00
H. H. Taylor, Gilded, Patent Regulator, Adjusted..... 25 00
G. M. Wheeler, Nickel, Patent Regulator............. 18 00
G. M. Wheeler, Gilded, Patent Regulator 17 00

18 SIZE, STEM WIND, HUNTING, NAMELESS.

No. 27. Nickel, Expansion Balance, Adjusted, 15 Jewels in Settings, Patent Regulator, Breguet Hair Spring, Double Sunk Dial $40 00
No. 70 Gilded, Expansion Balance, Adjusted, 15 Jewels in Settings, Patent Regulator, Breguet Hair Spring, Double Sunk Dial 35 00
No. 33. Nickel, Same as H. H. Taylor, Pat. Reg., Adj... 30 00
No. 80. Gilded, Same as H. H. Taylor, Pat. Reg., Adj ... 25 00
No. 103. Nickel, Same as G. M. Wheeler, Pat. Reg 18 00
No. 82. Gilded, Same as G. M. Wheeler, Pat. Reg...... 17 00
No. 102. Half Nickel, 11 Jewels...................... 14 00
No. 10. Gilded, 11 Jewels 12 50
No. 96. Gilded, 7 Jewels 10 00

18 SIZE, STEM WIND, PENDANT SET.

OPEN FACE ONLY.

B. W. Raymond, Gilded, Patent Regulator, Adjusted....$35 00
H. H. Taylor, Gilded, Patent Regulator, Adjusted............. 25 00
G. M. Wheeler, Gilded, Patent Regulator.................. 17 00
G. M. Wheeler, Full Nickel, Patent Regulator 18 00
No. 44. Full Nickel, Same as G. M. Wheeler, Pat. Reg.... 18 00
No. 76. Gilded, Same as H. H. Taylor, Pat. Reg......... 25 00
No. 75. Gilded, Same as G. M. Wheeler, Pat. Reg....... 17 00
No. 43. Half Nickel, 11 Jewels.......................... 14 00
No. 74. Expansion Balance, 11 Jewels....................... 12 50
No. 73. Expansion Balance, 7 Jewels.................... 10 00

18 SIZE, KEY WIND.

No. 97. Gilded, 7 Jewels $7 00

16 SIZE, STEM WIND, ¾ PLATE,

FOR HUNTING ONLY.

No. 4. Nickel, Expansion Balance. Adjusted, 15 Jewels, 4 pairs Settings...... .... $40 00
No. 3. Gilded, Expansion Balance. Adjusted, 15 Jewels, 4 Pairs Settings 31 00
No. 2. Gilded, Expansion Balance, 13 Jewels, 3 Pairs Settings.................... 20 00
No. 92. Gilded, Expansion Balance, 11 Jewels........... 13 50

16 SIZE, STEM WIND, INTERCHANGEABLE.

FOR HUNTING OR OPEN FACE.

No. 72. Nickel, Compensation Balance, Adjusted to Heat, Cold, Isochronism and Position, 21 Jewels in raised Gold Settings, Breguet Hair Spring, Patent Regulator $170 00
No. 50. Nickel, Expansion Balance, Adjusted, 15 Jewels, Patent Regulator, 4 Pairs Settings................. 55 00

16 SIZE, S. W. BRIDGE, INTERCHANGEABLE.

No. 91. Nickel, Compensation Balance, Fully Adjusted, Patent Regulator....................$180 00
No. 86. Nickel, Expansion Balance, Adjusted, 15 Jewels, Patent Regulator, 4 Pairs Settings.................... 64 00

16 SIZE, STEM WIND, PENDANT SET.

OPEN FACE ONLY.

No. 108. Nickel, Expansion Balance, Adjusted, 15 Jewels, 4 Pairs Settings....................$40 00
No. 107. Gilded, Expansion Balance, Adjusted, 15 Jewels, 4 Pairs Settings.................... 31 00
No. 106. Gilded, Expansion Balance, 13 Jewels, 3 Pairs Settings.................... 20 00
No. 105. Gilded, Expansion Balance, 11 Jewels............. 13 50
No. 104. Gilded, Expansion Balance, 7 Jewels............. 10 00

6 SIZE, STEM WIND, NAMELESS.

No. 71. Nickel, Expansion Balance, Firmly Adjusted, 17 Jewels in raised Gold Settings, Breguet Hair Spring.....$60 00
No. 67. Nickel, Expansion Balance, 15 Jewels, 4 Pairs.... 27 00
No. 45. Nickel, 13 Jewels (3 Pairs in Settings)............. 20 00
No. 101. Nickel, 11 Jewels 15 50
No. 94. Expansion Balance, 11 Jewels............. 14 50
No. 95. Expansion Balance, 7 Jewels.................... 12 00

All 18 Size Movements are Full Plate. For Cases to fit same, see other pages.
Refer to our Pocket Net Lists for any changes that may occur in above or any other Movements.
We guarantee Market Prices in every instance.

Elgin movements from an 1889 catalog.

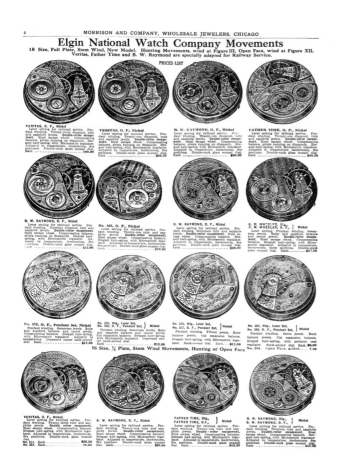

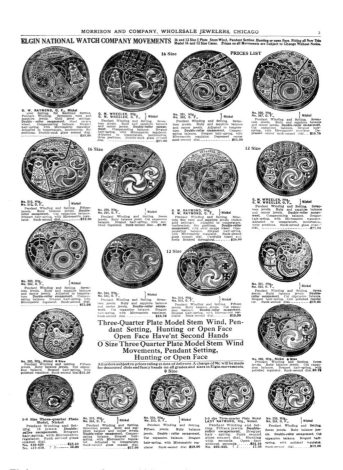

Elgin movements from a 1917 catalog.

Elgin movements from a 1917 catalog.

Gruen, Veri-Thin, circa 1920s, 17J, GF, five-sided case, $175-$475.

Gruen, Veri-Thin, movement view.

Gruen, Veri-Thin Swiss, circa 1910, fancy engraved metal dial, GF, $200-$350.

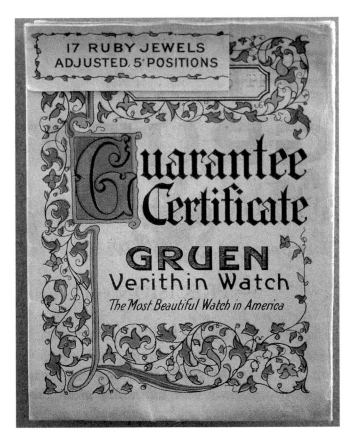

Gruen, Veri-Thin, original papers.

Gruen, Veri-Thin with copper dial, circa 1930s, 15J, GF, $100-$200.

Gruen, Veri-Thin, 15J, movement view.

Hamilton Watch Co., Lancaster, Pennsylvania

Founded in 1892, this company is regarded by many collectors as the overall premier watch manufacturer in American history. The company produced high-quality watches and was very popular in the railroad industry. The master watchmaker I worked for in the 1970s timed every watch that left the store up against a Hamilton 992B pocket watch that hung on a nail in the watch repair room. Hamilton made watchmaking history when it introduced its electric battery-powered wrist watch in 1957. Hamilton railroad pocket watches are sought after by collectors, as are examples from the very large wrist-watch line that it produced.

Hamilton 946, Parks Jewelers-Dauphine, Manitoba, Canada, circa 1905, 23J 18 size, $695-$1,195.

Hamilton, 946 movement view.

Hamilton, circa 1897, Montgomery dial, 24-hour division inside hour chapter, 14kt HC, 17J 18 size, $595-$1,095.

Hamilton, 17J 18 size movement.

Hamilton, Grade 944, circa 1905, 19J 18 size, five position, display type case, $275-$575.

Hamilton, 19J movement.

Hamilton, 14kt HC.

Hamilton 950, circa 1906, 23J 16 size, movement view, $795-$1,295.

Hamilton 992, circa 1907, 21J 16 size movement, $295-$595.

Hamilton, 992, RR movement.

Hamilton, 992, circa 1909, 21J 16 size, silver case, $295-$595.

Hamilton, circa 1919, 992 Time King, 21J 16 size, $295-$595.

Hamilton, Model 992L, circa 1932, 21J 16 size, WGF, signed Ham., case with solid bow, $395-$895.

Hamilton, 992 movement.

Hamilton RR, 992B, circa 1942, 21J 16 size, YGF, signed Ham. case, $395-$795.

Hamilton, 992B movement.

Hamilton, 992B Railway Special, circa 1942, 21J, GF, two-tone case, $325-$625.

Hamilton, chronograph/Grade 23, circa WW II, nickel plate, $295-$495.

Hamilton, 4992B, GCT (Greenwich Civil Time), circa 1942, 22J, chrome case/24-hour black dial, $395-$595.

Hamilton, 4992B movement, Greenwich Civil Time.

Hamilton, circa 1940s, military Grade 23 chronograph, 19J 16 size, unusual refinished white dial, $295-$495.

Hamilton Watch Company

HERE'S A WATCH
THAT KNOWS ITS BUSINESS

Railroad Model No. 2

10K filled Yellow Gold $60

And Its Business is Keeping Railroad Men on Time

How many men on your run carry Hamiltons? Ask them what they think of this watch of railroad accuracy. They'll tell you what the engineers of famous fliers like the **Broadway Limited**, the **Twentieth Century**, and the **Crescent**—have said as they pose with their Hamiltons in their hands: **"Here's a watch that knows its business!"**

That's why, if you are considering a new watch, it will pay you to drop in at our conveniently located store and see the Hamilton railroad models. Buy a Hamilton, carry it year after year and you'll know the feeling of confidence inspired by the ownership of a watch you can depend upon.

The watch shown is the famous Hamilton 992—railroad model No. 2, in dust-proof case with the non-pull-out stem protector.

Hamilton 1929 ad.

Hamilton, Grade 912, circa 1938, 12 size, engraved metal dial, GF, $75-$175.

Hamilton, Grade 917 with box, circa 1937, 17J 10 size, GF, $125-$295.

Hamilton, 917 movement, 10 size.

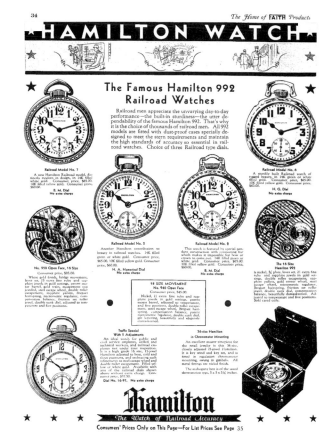

992 railroad watches, 1931.

The masterpiece group.

Hamilton Grade 912 watches.

HAMILTON WATCH MOVEMENT ILLUSTRATIONS

18 SIZE

GRADE 936

Open face, 17 jewels, single roller
before No. 426001, double roller
after No. 426000

GRADE 925

Hunting, 17 jewels, single roller

16 SIZE

GRADE 974

Open face, ¾ plate movt., 17 jewels,
single roller before No. 247001,
double roller after No. 247000

GRADE 992

Open face, ¾ plate movt., 21 jewels,
single roller before No. 377001,
double roller after No. 379000

GRADE 992B

Open face, ¾ plate movt.,
21 jewels, double roller

GRADE 950

Open face, bridge movt.,
23 jewels, double roller

GRADE 950B

Open face, bridge movt.,
23 jewels, double roller

Hamilton watch movement illustrations.

Hampden Watch Co., Canton, Ohio

Founded in the late 1870s, this company produced watches, the vast majority being pocket type, up until the early 1930s when it was bought by the Russians, who used the company to start watch manufacturing in that country.

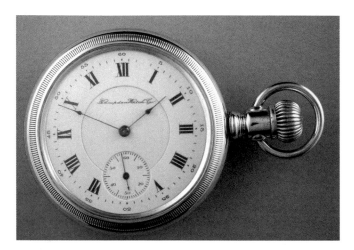

Hampden, circa 1903, 21J 16 size, display-type case, nickel case double sunk dial, $175-$375.

Hampden, 21J 16 size, HC sidewinder movement.

Hampden, circa 1917, 21J 16 size, Montgomery dial, GF, $295-$495.

Hampden, 21 J 16 size movement, Grade 105.

Hampden, the "Minuteman," circa 1920, 17J 12 size, white gold-filled case two-tone dial, $90-$290.

Hampden, 17 J 12 size, "Minute Man" movement.

Hampden, Duber, circa 1918, 17J 12 size "Paul Revere" movement, WGF, $90-$290.

Hampden, 17J 12 size, "Paul Revere" movement.

Hampden case back.

Hampden, circa 1891, 6 size, 14kt multicolor HC, $500-$1,000.

Hampden movement.

Hampden, case front, green and pink gold, flowers and parrot motif.

Hebdomas, Swiss, exposed balance, silver and Niello case, fancy dial, $395-$595.

E. Howard & Co., Boston, Massachusetts

Edward Howard, a pioneer in American watch history, produced excellent pocket watches with his company. Complete watches in their original cases are extremely collectible and sought after. The company was sold to the Keystone Watchcase Company in 1903. It continued producing fine quality pocket watches until 1930.

E Howard & Co., Boston, circa 1870s, N size (approx. 18 size), transition period pendant set, 18kt HC, $1,500-$2,800.

E Howard & Co., Boston, N size (approx. 18 size) movement.

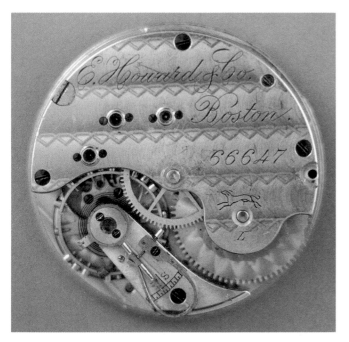

E Howard & Co., Boston, L size (approx. 16 size), circa 1880s, movement only, $350.

E. Howard Watch Co. Movement, 1889. E. Howard Watch Co. (Keystone Watch Case Co.), Waltham, Massachusetts, 1903-1930.

Howard-Keystone, circa 1910, 21J 16 size, nickel display-type case, $295-$595.

Howard-Keystone, 16 size 21J movement.

Howard-Keystone, Series 11, circa 1913, 21J 16 size, $395-$795.

Howard, Series 11 movement view.

Inside case back.

Howard R.R. Watches

Treat yourself to a Howard

The Howard Railroad Chronometer is a 16 size, 21 Jewel lever set movement, closely adjusted to 5 pos., heat, cold and isochronism.

The 23 Jewel movement and the 21 Jewel Series No. 10 movement have selected rubies and sapphires with oriental sapphire pallet stones and banking pins. Train and balance have olive hole-jewels. Recessed steel escape wheel. Closely adjusted to 5 pos., heat, cold and isochronism.

Howard Railroad Watches are fitted in the famous Keystone Railroad Case with many special features. The pendant is spun on the center. Heavy stock, long thread on the screws. Narrow bezel with bead gives more hand room under the glass. Dust proof Nut Pendant, *Non pull-out Bow*

MONTGOMERY DIALS SUPPLIED ON HOWARD RAILROAD
WATCHES ON REQUEST WITHOUT EXTRA CHARGE

◆

Every Howard movement is fitted and timed in its own case at the factory

11

Howard-Keystone, circa 1912, RR swing-out case, 21J Series 11 movement, $395-$795.

Howard RR watches.

Illinois Watch Co., Springfield, Illinois

Founded in 1869, this prolific company turned out to be the third largest producer behind Elgin and Waltham in terms of numbers of jeweled watches produced. In 1927, the company was sold to Hamilton. Its fine quality pocket watches were very popular among railroadmen, and the line of wrist watches it produced is highly collectible.

Illinois movement.

Illinois, circa 1880, 18 size, silver, very rare floral dial, $595-$995.

Illinois, Bunn Special, circa 1903, 24J 18 size, movement view, $1,000-$1,500.

Illinois, circa 1896, 18 size, display case, 17J two-tone checkerboard movement, Chalmer pat. Regulator, $195-$395.

Illinois, 18 size movement view.

Illinois, Bunn Special, circa 1904, 24J 18 size, silver swing-out case, $1,000-$1,500.

Illinois, case back train scene.

Washington Watch Co., Illinois "Liberty Bell," circa 1906, 17J 18 size, OF nickel case, $100-$300.

Washington Watch Co., Illinois movement.

Illinois, "Locomotive," circa 1887, 11J 18 size KW transition, 4 oz OF silver case, $295-$595.

Illinois, 11J KW movement, locomotive on movement.

Illinois Sagamo, circa 1902, 23J 16 size, two-tone movement, $795-$1,295.

23J two-tone movement.

Illinois, Bunn Special, circa 1923, 23J 16 size, nickel swing-out case, $600-$1,200.

Illinois, Bunn Special movement.

Illinois, Sagamo Special, circa 1925, 23J, solid bow, $895-$1,395.

Sagamo Special, movement view.

Illinois, Bunn Special, 60 hours, circa 1928, WGF, 21J 16 size, $350-$750.

Illinois, 21J movement, RR, 60-hour Bunn Special.

Illinois, Bunn Special, Grade 161A, circa 1938, 21J 16 size GF, movement view, $1,000-$2,000.

Inside case back.

Illinois, Santa Fe Special, circa 1923, 21J 16 size, $495-$995.

Santa Fe Special movement.

Illinois, fancy GF hunter case, rare fancy dial with butterfly, 16 size, $595-$995.

Illinois, circa 1910, 17 J, three-finger bridge, $100-$225.

Illinois, Burlington Special 16 size, circa 1910, 19J adj., GF, $150-$350.

Illinois, Burlington Special, three-finger bridge movement.

Illinois, Sears and Roebuck Special, circa 1902, 17J 16 size, $125-$250.

Illinois movement, Sears and Roebuck Special.

Illinois, Grade 706, circa 1928, 16 size 17J adj. to four positions, WGF, $195-$395.

Illinois, Grade 706, 17J adj to four-position movement.

Illinois pocket watch ads.

Illinois pocket watch ads.

THE ILLINOIS WATCH

The Marquis Autocrat Pocket Series
17 Jewel Thin Watches

These fine 17 jewel watches are splendid values. Smartly attractive and of modern design, they are truly representative of fine Illinois workmanship. The Marquis Autocrat series have all the advantages of Illinois design and accuracy. Each is a 17 jewel timekeeper adjusted to 3 positions.

The DEAN
A solid gold pocket watch of distinguished appearance. 14K solid white gold case with inside cap. *Suggested consumer price, $65.*

The TRUSTEE
A new and distinctive watch design is achieved in the Trustee, with its seven sided case and inlaid green and black enamel back. 14K white or natural filled gold. *Suggested consumer price, $55.*

The CUSHION
Smartly designed and of proven worth. Truly a fine pocket watch, 14K white filled gold, plain or engraved case. *Suggested consumer price, $55.*

The RIALTO
A thin watch of unusual beauty. 14K white or green filled gold. Plain or engraved back case. *Suggested consumer price, $50.*

The OXFORD
Rich, dignified and with a quiet simplicity. This is one of the finest of the Marquis-Autocrat series. 14K white or green filled gold. *Suggested consumer price, $50*

The ETON
A handsome watch with character in its design. 14K white filled gold. *Suggested consumer price, $50.*

* * *

Regular 12 Size Watches

Produced to meet the exacting tastes of those who desire a medium priced watch that may be depended upon for accuracy and durability. It is fully guaranteed to be thoroughly reliable. The 17 Jewel Autocrat and the 19 jewel Dorian are both unusually fine watches and are real watch values.

The AUTOCRAT
Accuracy and dependability are built into this fine 17 jewel watch. 14K white or green filled gold. *Suggested consumer price, $43.50.*

The DORIAN
The Dorian Razor-Second dial is a great help in actually timing by seconds. This 19 jewel watch is in 14K white or natural filled gold. *Suggested consumer price, $55.* With Regular Dial, $50

Ad from a 1931 catalog.

THE ILLINOIS WATCH

The Distinguished Lincoln Series
19 Jewel Thin Pocket Watches

Striking proof of fine watch craftsmanship—The Illinois Lincoln series watches represent the finest in time-accuracy and design. Their luxurious simplicity,—their perfection in every detail, their life and color, portray the hand of the master artist. Each Illinois Lincoln is a 19 jeweled, 12 size thin watch.

The DIRECTOR
Fashioned in solid gold with a beautiful hand carved pattern of distinction. The Director is a most appropriate presentation watch for it will give a lifetime of accurate service. 14K solid white gold. Hand carved case with Butler back. Sterling silver dial with 18K applied numerals. *Suggested consumer price, $110.*

The TRUSTEE
This watch is exceptionally popular—because of its unusual design and simplicity. The plain back of the Trustee has beautiful pattern of inlaid green enamel for monogram. 14K white or natural filled gold. *Suggested consumer price, $75.*

The DEAN
The most beautiful watch of the Lincoln series. Its simplicity gives it an unusual richness and dignity. The case and bow harmonize perfectly giving the Dean splendid design balance. The Dean case is fashioned from 14K solid white gold. *Suggested consumer price, $100.*

The PIONEER
This beautifully thin watch is available in a number of case designs. 14K White or green filled gold with Butler, etched or lined backs. *Suggested consumer price, $75.*

The CUSHION
The Cushion shape is an extremely popular one for fine pocket watch. 14K white filled gold. Plain or oxidized case. *Suggested consumer price, $75.*

The BOURSE
A new pocket watch of harmonious design. 14K white or green filled gold. Butler or lined backs. *Suggested consumer price, $75.*

Ad from a 1931 catalog.

Illinois movement from an 1890's catalog.

THE ILLINOIS WATCH

Illinois Uncased Watches
16 Size » » 17 and 19 Jewels

Illinois uncased watches are all high-grade dependable timepieces. They may readily be fitted in standard size cases of any design.

For years, wholesale and retail jewelers have recognized the superiority of Illinois uncased watches and have used them in large numbers to provide their stock with an unlimited case design selection.

NO. 169   19 JEWELS   16 SIZE
Open face   LS or PS
19 Jewels; adjusted to temperature and three positions; spring tempered compensating balance; double roller escapement; sapphire jewels; steel escape wheel; rounded arm train wheels; gold center wheel; Breguet hairspring; patent regulator; recoil click; Double sink or silvered dial. *Suggested consumer price, $32.50.*

NO. 167   17 JEWELS   16 SIZE
Open face   LS or PS
17 jewels; polished settings; adjusted to temperature; hardened compensating balance; double roller escapement; steel escape wheel; rayed center wheel; Breguet hairspring; patent micrometric screw regulator; safety pinion; rayed winding wheels; safety recoil click; white enamel or silvered dial. *Suggested consumer price, $24*

12 Size » » 17, 19 and 21 Jewels

19 JEWELS   NO. 129   OPEN FACE
19 jewels; adjusted to temperature and three positions; spring tempered compensating balance; double roller escapement; sapphire jewels; steel escape wheel; rounded arm train wheels; gold center wheel; Breguet hairspring; recoil click. *Suggested consumer price, $32.50.*

21 JEWEL   NO. 321   OPEN FACE
21 jewels; adjusted to temperature and 3 positions; compensating balance; double roller escapement; steel escape wheel; sapphire jewels; gold strata beveled and polished center wheel; Breguet hairspring; patent regulator; safety pinion; concaved and polished winding wheels; recoil click; damaskened in a striped pattern. *Suggested consumer price, $40.*

17 JEWELS   NO. 127   OPEN FACE
17 jewels; oreide settings; adjusted to temperature; spring tempered compensating balance; double roller escapement; steel escape wheel; sapphire jewels; rayed center wheel; Breguet hairspring; patent micrometric screw regulator; safety pinion; rayed winding wheels; safety recoil click; damaskened in a striped pattern. *Suggested consumer price, $25.*

3-0 Size » » 17 Jewels

NO. 307   HUNTING   17 JEWELS
Bridge Model
17 Ruby and sapphire jewels; steel escape wheel; Breguet hairspring; micrometric screw regulator; safety recoil click. *Suggested consumer price, $30*

18-0 Size » » 17 Jewels

The Illinois 3/0 size movement has an illustrious history. It was selected by the United States Government for use during the late war. During the 1929 Indianapolis race 10 watches containing this movement were strapped to the wrists of the leading drivers—and, every one of them came through the race—still keeping accurate time. The Illinois 18/0 movement is available for use in diamond set cases only. It must be cased at the Illinois factory.

Size Eighteen-O or six and three-fourths ligne, 17 ruby and sapphire jewels, safety recoiling click, double roller escapement, tempered and hardened compensating balance, steel escape wheel, concaved and polished winding wheels.

Ad from a 1931 catalog.

Ingersoll (Robert H. Ingersoll & Bro.), New York, New York

Founded in 1881, it produced inexpensive, non-jeweled, "dollar" watches. When competition became fierce among watch companies, Ingersoll sold its watches for $1.

Ingersoll, Reliance, circa 1894, 16 size 7J, nickel, $50-$100.

Ingersoll, Reliance, 16 size 7J movement.

102   THE HOROLOGICAL REVIEW.   May 12, 1906

IMPORTANT TO KNOW!

Every jeweler who even pretends to keep abreast of affairs in his trade should know this about the most prominently advertised watch before the public to-day—

The "I-T" is an entirely reconstructed and improved product absolutely superior to **any** 7-jewel watch heretofore on the market, regardless of price or reputation. If this is true—and an examination will prove it—should you not be informed about it? The coupon below will bring the evidence.

(1) Sold only direct to the retail trade.

(2) Only responsible jewelers can handle them.

(3) Retail prices absolutely restricted.

ROBT. H. INGERSOLL & BRO.
45 John St., New York
I am willing to know about the Ingersoll-Trenton watch and its trade policies.

NAME

STREET

TOWN

ROBT. H. INGERSOLL & BRO.
HOME OFFICE: 45 JOHN STREET, NEW YORK

Ingersoll movement ad.

Le Coultre-Swiss, circa 1940s, pocket alarm, brushed
aluminum, $400-$700.

Le Coultre pocket alarm in box.

Lemania-Swiss, chronograph, circa 1930s, black military dial,
chrome case, $495-$895.

Lemania movement, Swiss.

Longines, Switzerland

Longines, circa 1878, IIJ, nickel, $95-$295.

Longines movement.

Longines-Swiss, circa 1885, HC LS, 800 silver, $250-$450.

Longines case front with fob.

Longines inside case, Longines logo.

Longines movement.

The first Longines watch, caliber 840 hand-winding mechanical movement, circa 1867, HC silver pocket watch, white dial inscribed with 12 Roman numerals, sub-seconds at 6 o' clock. Photo courtesy Longines Museum Collection.

Circa 1920 19-ligne minute repeater movement, chronograph, enameled 18kt HC with gold dial, Breguet-style numerals. Photo courtesy Longines Museum Collection.

Circa 1919 HC set with diamonds, rubies and emeralds, personalized with a monogram, dial enhanced with painted Arabic numerals. Photo courtesy Longines Museum Collection.

Movado, Switzerland

In 1881, Achille Ditesheim, barely 19 years old and fresh out of watchmaking school, founded his own watchmaking company and was soon joined by three of his brothers. In 1905, a new modern factory was built and a new company name was introduced: Movado. Movado means "always in motion" in the international language of Esperanto—a language based on words with roots commonly found in the romance languages. Esperanto was very popular among cosmopolitan circles throughout Europe, providing an interesting insight into the Ditesheim's vision for its company.

In the first decade of the 20th century, when the market was still geared to pocket watches, Movado advanced the development of the wrist-watch movement. The company was regarded as a pioneer in miniaturized movements and in 1912 introduced the Polyplan watch. An ultimate in conception, design, and engineering, Polyplan housed one of the earliest patented "form" movements, constructed on three planes inside a curved case that followed the natural contours of the wrist. In 1926, the company launched a new watch design called the Ermeto. One of the most unusual watches ever created, this unique pillow-shaped pocket watch housed a patented movement that was wound by the sliding motion of the case as it was opened and closed. The sections of the two-part metal case opened like curtains to reveal the dial. A single opening provided sufficient winding of the mainspring for four hours running time; with six openings, it would run all day and night. The name "Ermeto" was derived from the Greek word meaning "sealed."

Although not actually air or water tight, the term suggested protection against shock, dust, and temperature changes. Carried loose or attached to a chain, Ermeto was known as the only watch suitable for both men and women—a novel concept at the time. The 1930s were productive years for Movado. The factory developed its two-button Chronograph wrist watches with calendar indications that even included moon phases. Movado began production of wrist watches with automatic winding in 1945, and in 1946 it introduced the Calendomatic. These self-winding wrist watches of the 1940s are still among the most nostalgic collectibles ever produced by Movado. The next technological advancement in automatic watches came in 1956 with the introduction of the Kingmatic, a series of rotor-driven timepieces.

A prophetic moment for Movado occurred in 1947 when Nathan George Horwitt, an adherent of the Bauhaus design movement and one of America's outstanding designers, set out to simplify the wrist watch. His solution was to become a legend in modern design known as the Movado Museum Watch. "We do not know time as a number sequence," he said, "but by the position of the sun as the earth rotates." Applying this theory, he eliminated the numerals from the dial. Strongly influenced by the clean, spare lines of the Bauhaus, he designed a dial defined by a single gold dot symbolizing the sun at high noon, the hands suggesting the movement of the earth.

Horwitt's prototype was selected by the Museum of Modern Arts in 1959 for its permanent collection. The name, the Museum Watch, is so integral to the company's image that to many it is the first timepiece that comes to mind when they think of Movado.

View of the Movado factory in La Chaux-de-Fonds, circa 1955. Photo courtesy of Movado Watch Co.

Portrait of Nathan George Horwitt, designer of the Movado Museum Watch. Photo courtesy of Movado Watch Co.

Movado, chronometer, circa 1920s, 18kt gold, $2,400-$3,000.

Movado, circa 1930s, metal dial, gold applied numbers, $150-$400.

Movado, circa 1930, Swiss steel case.

Movado inside case back, stamp with hand-holding pocket watch.

Two Movado deck watches in original test cases. Photo courtesy of Movado Watch Co.

Movado, small gold hunter case, enamel painting on front and back, white enamel dial, small seconds. Photo courtesy of Movado Watch Co.

Movado, decorated Art Deco, circa 1925, 18kt. Photo courtesy of Movado Watch Co.

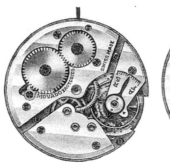

Two Movado pocket-watch movements.

Movado, minute repeating calendar chronograph, circa 1905, 18kt hunter case. Photo courtesy of Movado Watch Co.

Movado Ermeto ad, circa 1930s.

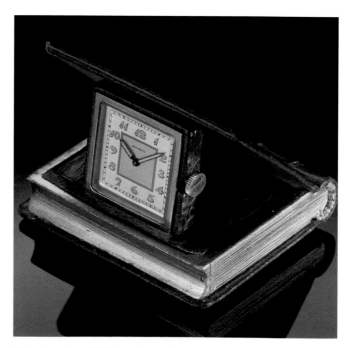

Movado, circa 1935, watch set in brown leather-bound book titled *Livre d' Heures*, caliber 150 MN movement. Photo courtesy Movado Watch Co.

Ulysse Nardin, Switzerland

Founded in 1846, this renowned company is known for its early high-precision marine chronometers. In 1935, Ulysse Nardin developed the caliber 22-24, the first Chronometer with splits second fly-back hands measuring 1/10th of a second. Used at the Berlin Olympic Games in 1936, they earned the company many Gold medals and Grand Prix prizes for their accuracy and perfection. This company still produces extremely high-quality complicated watches to this day.

Ulysse Nardin, engraved case inscribed "US Corp of Engineers, USA No. 9267."

Ulysse Nardin, HC chronograph, circa late 1800s, $1,500-$2,000.

Ulysse Nardin-Swiss, circa 1910s, enamel dial radium numbers, silver, $450-$750.

Pocket chronometer-chronograph, made for the Chicago Exhibition of 1893, 18kt and silver.

New Haven (New Haven Clock Co.)

New Haven, Connecticut, 1853-1946

New Haven, examples of the Tip-Top, $25-$75.

Omega, Switzerland

Omega, Philippine Expedition, circa 1899, caliber 19, enamel artwork. Photo courtesy of Omega.

Non-Magnetic Watch Co., Swiss made for American market, circa 1890s, 16 size, nickel, $150-$300.

16 size movement view.

Omega, Gurzelen Watch Co., circa 1895, silver case, railroad locomotive engraving. Photo courtesy of Omega.

Omega, circa 1930s, 15J, unusual stainless case, $250-$450.

Omega-Swiss, circa 1974, stainless steel, hacking feature, $195-$395.

Omega, movement view.

Patek Philippe, Switzerland

Founded in 1839 and considered to be one of the most important watchmakers in the world, this high-end company produced, and still creates, incredible works of the watchmaking art. These watches are built to last and have been purchased throughout its 160-plus-year history by notables the likes of Queen Victoria, Kipling, Einstein, Tolstoy, and Marie Curie to name but some. Every Patek is collectible.

Patek Philippe, A.H. Rodanet & Co. Paris, circa 1870s, 18kt, Roman numerals, $2,000-$3,000.

Patek Philippe, Switzerland, movement view.

Patek Philippe, Shreve & Co., circa 1896, 18kt pink gold case, unusual sweep second, $2,500-$3,500.

Patek Philippe, Switzerland, movement view.

Patek Philippe & Cie, circa 1920s, 18kt, 18J-gold metal dial, $2,000-$3,000.

Patek Philippe, Switzerland.

Patek Philippe & Cie, presentation watch, circa 1920s, 18kt, 18J, $2,000-$3,000.

Patek Philippe-Switzerland, Shreve & Co., San Francisco, California.

Patek Philippe, R. J. Richards Co., Massachusetts, circa 1920s, 18kt, 18J 8 adj., $2,000-$3,000.

Patek Philippe, movement view.

Patek Philippe, ladies pendant monogrammed case, circa 1900, 12 Ligne 18kt HC, $1,800-$2,500.

Patek case, dust cover view.

Patek movement.

Rockford Watch Co. Rockford, Illinois, 1874-1915

Rockford Watch Co., circa 1880s, rare 24-hour dial, 18 size KW transition, $1,200-$1,700.

Rockford Watch Co., circa 1886, 15J 18 size, GF fancy engraved HC, $195-$395.

Rockford, 18 size movement.

Rockford, 18 size, fancy engraved case.

Rockford watch ad.

Rolex, simple recorder (stop watch), circa 1920s, chrome case, $200-$300.

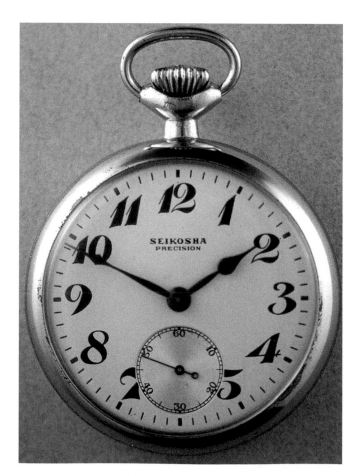

Seiko, Seikosha Precision, circa 1930s, 16 size, chrome case, $250-$500.

Early Seiko movement.

South Bend Watch Co., South Bend, Indiana, 1903-1929

South Bend, Grade 227 RR, circa 1928, 21J 16 size, double sunk dial, $250-$500.

South Bend, Grade 227, 21J 16 size RR.

South Bend Watch Co., OF Montgomery dial RR, $250-$500.

South Bend Watch Co., circa 1928, model 429, OF 12 size, $100-$200.

South Bend Watch Co., Studebaker, circa 1927, 21J 12 size, GF, $200-$400.

South Bend Watch Co.

Trenton Watch Co., circa 1891, HC LS, 7J 18 size, GF, $95-$295.

Trenton Watch Co., engraved case.

Trenton Watch Co., 7J movement.

THE SILENT SALESMAN

This is the reproduction of our electric flash-light window sign which has helped hundreds of jewelers to sell SOUTH BEND WATCHES. It helps to sell other lines of jewelry as well when it is placed in the window.

Every jeweler should have one of these signs. Write us for particulars of how to secure one of these wonderful signs.

South Bend Watch Co.
Manufacturers of High Grade Watches
SOUTH BEND, INDIANA

South Bend ad.

Hopalong Cassidy in box, U.S. Time Corp., circa approx. 1950s, PW OF, $150-$550.

Original Hopalong Cassidy box.

Vacheron Constantin-Switzerland

One of the oldest Swiss watch companies, tracing back to the 1700s, it has created some of the most beautiful watches the world has ever seen. Vacheron Constantin ranks among the top makers and is still in existence today. Its high-quality timepieces are extremely collectible and valuable.

Vacheron Constantin-Swiss, circa 1870s, 18kt fancy engraved HC, $1,750-$2,500.

Vacheron Constantin, fancy engraved case.

Vacheron Constantin-Swiss, presentation watch circa 1949, rare aluminum case, $1,500-$2,500.

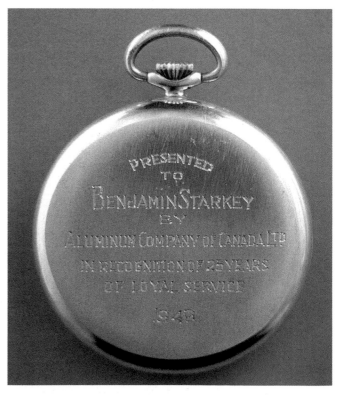

Vacheron Constantin-Swiss, presentation watch, inscribed case.

Waltham Watch Co. (American Waltham Watch Co.) Waltham, Massachusetts

This is the granddaddy of large American watch companies. Its beginnings are in the early 1850s and it produced high-quality watches of every grade. Early examples of Waltham timepieces are valuable collectors' items, and highly sought after. This company was always very innovative, and the pioneering spirit of the people who worked at Waltham led to the development of the machinery that built the watch industry in this country.

Waltham, 6 oz. massive case, PS Bartlett, circa 1870s, 15J 18 size, 6-oz coin silver HC, $350-$750.

Waltham, 6 oz. case back.

Waltham, Elk motif on case.

Waltham, circa 1884, 14kt Elk motif box hinge HC, 11J 18 size, $850-$1,650.

Waltham, Model 1883, circa 1888, GF OF 18 size, fancy dial-bird scene, $400-$700.

American Waltham, circa 1890s, 18 size, nickel case, fancy dial, $250-$550.

Waltham, Model 1883, circa 1887, 18 size Appleton Tracy movement, nickel display case, $125-$250.

Waltham, Model 1883, Appleton Tracy movement view.

Waltham, A.W.W. Co., circa 1896, nickel swing-out case, 7J 18 size gilt movement, $75-$175.

Waltham, circa 1888, 18 size, OF nickel display-type case, unusual white hairspring (normally blue steel hairspring), $125-$250.

Waltham, Model 1883, Canadian Pacific Railway, circa 1888, 17J 18 size, $500-$1,000.

Waltham, RR 17J, Canadian Pacific Railway, beaver logo, movement view.

Waltham "Santa Fe Route," circa 1892, 17J 18 size, $595-$1,195.

Santa Fe Route, movement view.

Waltham, unusual case back with engraving, balance exposed to show a bicycle wheel.

Waltham, circa 1903, Vanguard movement view, 19J 18 size, $175-$400.

Waltham, Vanguard up-down indicator, circa 1926, 23J RR, $600-$1,100.

Waltham, 23 J up-down indicator, movement view.

Waltham, Premier Vanguard, circa 1942, 23J 16 size, RR, GF, $200-$350.

Waltham Vanguard, movement view.

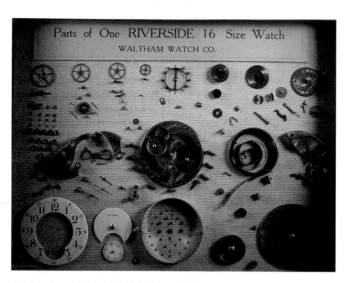

Parts of one Riverside 16 size watch.

Two thoroughbreds' ad.

Waltham, Riverside Maximus, circa 1901, 23J 16 size PS, $495-$995.

Waltham Riverside movement.

Waltham, 23 J Vanguard, movement view, circa 1904, 16 size, GF, $250-$550.

Waltham, Vanguard up-down indicator, GF 16 size, double sunk, bold dial, $600-$1,100.

Waltham Vanguard, circa 1902, 19J 16 size, double sunk dial, $150-$350.

Waltham Vanguard, 16 size 19J, movement view.

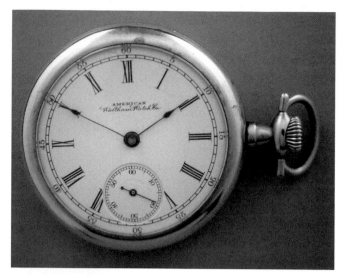

Waltham (A.W.W.Co.), Sidewinder, circa 1896, GF 16 size, 15J, $90-$150.

Waltham, 16 size 15J, movement view.

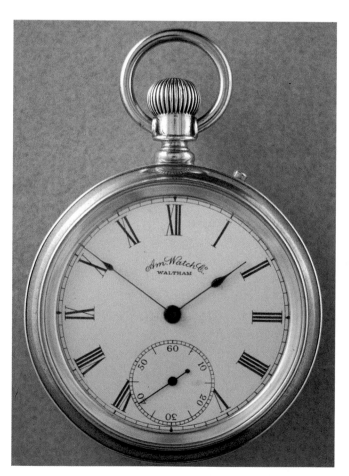

Waltham, Bond St., circa 1887, 16 size PS, coin silver, $150-$325.

Waltham, gilt movement view.

Waltham, fancy dial, GF OF, 16 size, $250-$350.

Waltham, circa 1885, 14 size, GF HC, fancy pink and green floral dial, $250-$700.

Waltham, circa 1885, LS, 6 size, 11J OF, 14kt, $150-$275.

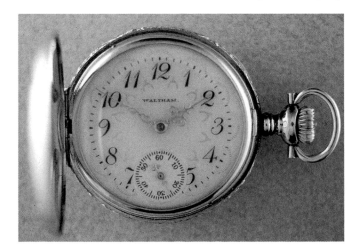

Waltham, circa 1905, 14kt HC, gold and enamel dial, 7J O size, $495-$795.

Waltham fancy case.

Waltham, circa 1887, 6 size LS 7J, 14kt, $150-$295.

Waltham case front view.

Waltham case back.

Waltham movement view.

Waltham movements, from an 1889 catalog.

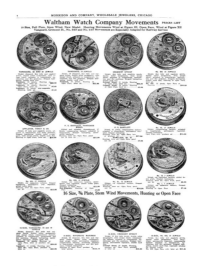

Waltham movements, from a 1917 catalog.

Waltham, circa 1912, 15J, 14kt HC, O size, $175-$375.

Waltham case front view.

Waltham case back.

Waltham movement view.

Waltham, 2/0 size, circa 1889, set with 76 diamonds on front and rear, enamel portrait hand painted on case back, high grade movement, $3,500-$5,000.

Waltham, enamel portrait hand-painted on case.

Waltham, 2/0 size, high grade movement.

Waterbury Watch Co., Addison Series N, circa 1890s, duplex escapement, silver case, $75-$95.

Waterbury Watch Co., Addison movement.

Wyler-Swiss, The Skipper, circa 1950s, 17J incaflex, chrome case, $75-$150.

Zenith Swiss, unusual alarm pocket watch, PS circa 1910s, nickel case-enamel dial, missing hand, $300-$450.

Miscellaneous Swiss Watches

J. W. Allen, 37 Strand London, circa 1875, oversize Swiss movement, PS, $250-$450.

Bucherer Swiss, circa 1950s, 17J, stainless, $175-$375.

B.W.C. Chronometer, Swiss, chrome plated, $150-$250.

L. Chopard, high grade Swiss movement, $300-$600.

Dauntless, Swiss, 18kt ornate HC, $400-$600.

Duo-style sterling purse watch, circa 1920s-1930s, green enamel sapphire pusher, $200-$300.

Duo-style purse watch open.

Eterna Swiss, circa 1920s, silver niello, $350-$550.

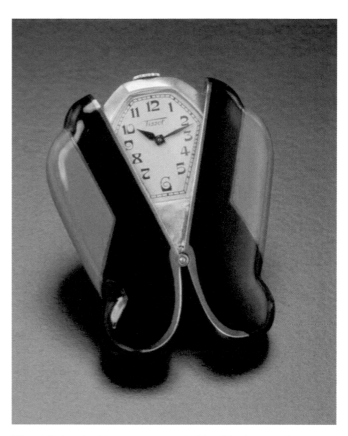

Tissot Swiss Art Deco purse watch, blue-black enamel, $193-$395.

Eterna purse watch, sterling, circa 1930, $195-$395.

Eterna purse watch, fold-out lid reveals watch.

Ermeto purse watch closed.

Movado Ermeto, circa 1940s, purse watch, small size-leather, $195-$395.

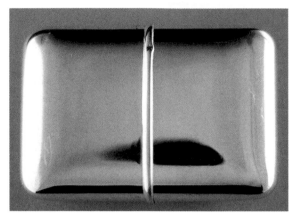

Movado Ermeto Chronometer, circa 1930s, sterling silver gold wash, winds as you open and close the case, $295-$495.

Movado Ermeto purse watch open.

Swiss sterling purse watch, circa 1920s-1930s, sapphire crown, $150-$250.

Swiss sterling purse watch open.

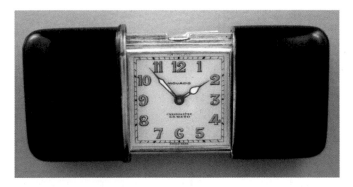

Movado Ermeto Chronometer, opening and closing winds movement, black enamel-purse watch, $295-$495.

Ermeto with diamonds, blue enamel, circa 1930. Photo courtesy of Movado Watch Co.

Swiss Stratford, Langendorf movement, circa 1920s, 6J, GF, $75-$175.

Unusual enamel and gold dial, gun metal case, $95-$195.

Swiss Minute Repeater, circa 1890s, 18kt gold HC, $3,500-$5,500.

Minute Repeater dust cover.

Minute Repeater movement.

Swiss, circa 1910s, eight-day, visible balance, nickel silver, $150-$250.

Unusual Swiss, exposed movement, circa 1930s, $300-$400.

Swiss, eight-day movement.

Duplex heavily engraved movement.

Swiss, 14kt gold HC, $700-$1,200.

Swiss HC back.

Fancy old pedometer, interesting dial, circa 1890s, $75-$150.

Duplex, circa 1870s, made for the Chinese market, fancy enamel dial/engraved movement, sweep second with mock pendulum, $300-500.

Swiss, circa 1920s, rectangular sterling case, $250-$450.

Swiss digital, 1920s to 1930, base metal, $100-$200.

Chronometer lip, pin set, $195-$395.

Tissot repeater movement view. Photo courtesy of Tissot.

Tissot 18kt HC, Chronograph with minute-repeater, circa 1881.
Photo courtesy of Tissot.

Tissot repeater, dust-cover view. Photo courtesy of Tissot.

Examples of Niello Pocket Watches Circa 1900s-1920s

Niello is a form of black enamel decoration used mostly on silver watch cases. The designs are deeply engraved into the metal, then filled with the enamel mixture and heated. The silver, or gold inlay high spots, pick out the design. Niello-type cases were used by many fine watch companies such as Rolex, Eterna, and Omega. Depending on the condition, as niello is semi-hard and fragile, and whether it is a well-known watch brand, values are $250-$1,200 and up.

Niello case with car race scene.

Demi -hunter back.

Flowers with plate for engraving monogram.

Demi-hunter front.

Eterna.

Eterna checkerboard case back.

Oriental design.

Bird on branch.

Hunting scene on horseback.

Oriental beauty, gold head ornament.

Hunter case front-Lion.

Case back-Leopard.

Floral design.

Art Deco design.

Floral design.

Sunburst design.

Fancy two-tone case with emblem.

Woman with hair ornament, crackle background.

Fancy scroll design.

Jungle scene.

Examples of Repoussé Watches

Repoussé is a style of metalwork where the metal is hammered up from the reverse side to form a design. Depending on the subject portrayed, condition, and size of the case, these artful watches vary in price from $200 to $500 and up.

French, circa early 1900s, sterling-dragon scene.

Art Deco, woman, bird, and four-leaf clover.

Unusual shaped case, floral design.

Unusual shape case, back.

Ducks and dogs.

Case back, pointer.

Three dogs on case.

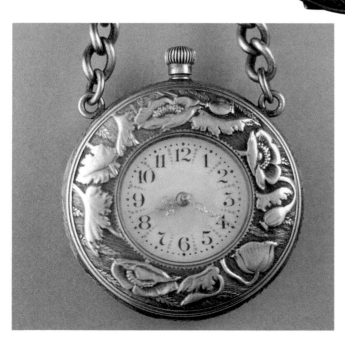

Silver repoussé case, poppy design.

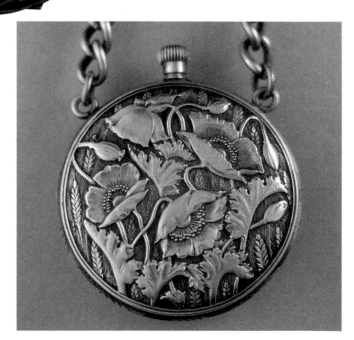

Case back, poppies.

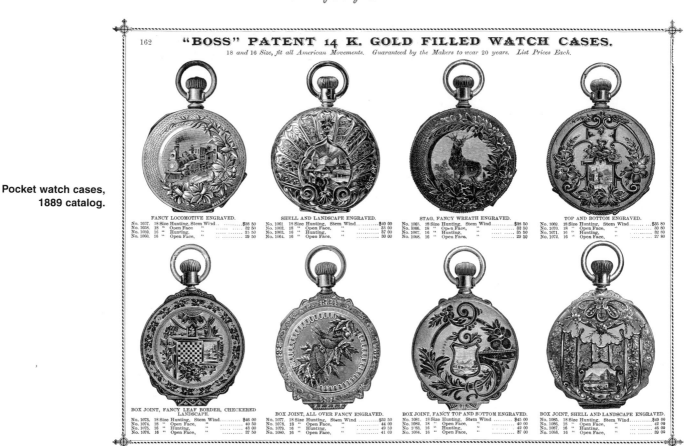

Pocket watch cases, 1889 catalog.

Pocket watch cases, 1917 catalog.

Wrist Watches

Benrus, circa 1920s-30s, square two tone, chrome with gold bezel, 15J, $95-$195.

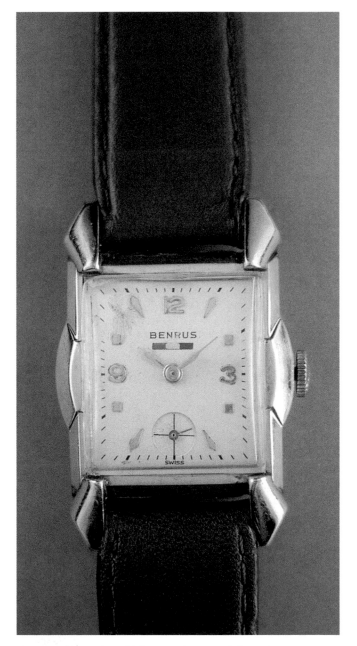

Benrus, circa 1940s, GF case, sub-seconds/large lugs, $95-$195.

Blancpain, Switzerland

Since 1735, Blancpain, the world's oldest watch brand, has symbolized the finest in traditional mechanical watch making. Through its famous slogan, "Since 1735, there has never been a quartz Blancpain watch, and there never will be," the brand has consistently made clear its determination to perpetuate this remarkable know-how, the pride of Swiss watch making.

In 1926, Blancpain contributed to watch history by producing the prototype of the first wrist watch with an "automatic"-wind mechanism, for the famous "Harwood," the invention of John Harwood an English horologist. In 1953, Blancpain released the "Fifty Fathoms." As one of the first diver watches to be water-resistant to 50 fathoms (300 feet), it would soon become a precious working tool for divers the world over. Jacques Cousteau and his divers wore this watch when they made the film, "The World of Silence," in 1956, and it was soon recognized and adopted by the armed forces of several nations, like the U.S. Navy and the French and German armies. This famous firm still produces mechanical watches to this day and is regarded as one of the top makers.

Fifty Fathoms divers' watches, stainless steel-automatic, circa 1950s, $1,500-$3,000.

Ernest Borel, circa 1950s, 18kt square case, $250-$500.

Bovet-Swiss, chronograph, two register, circa 1940s, stainless case with square pushers, $495-$895.

Navitimer, illustration, upper booklet.

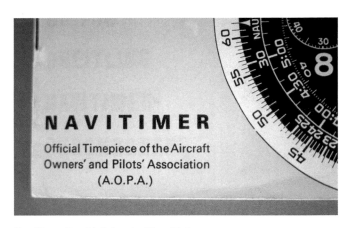

Navitimer Booklet, front of booklet.

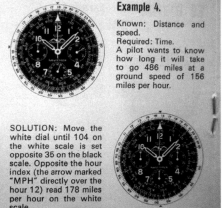

GROUND SPEED

The white and black scales are used for determination of ground speed problems. Two of the following quantities are available for its solution: time, distance, ground speed.

Example 3.

Known: Distance and Time.
Required: Ground speed.
A pilot finds by the use of check points that he has traveled 104 miles in 35 minutes.

Example 4.

Known: Distance and speed.
Required: Time.
A pilot wants to know how long it will take to go 486 miles at a ground speed of 156 miles per hour.

SOLUTION: Move the white dial until 104 on the white scale is set opposite 35 on the black scale. Opposite the hour index (the arrow marked "MPH" directly over the hour 12) read 178 miles per hour on the white scale.

Navitimer, illustration, ground speed.

SOLUTION: On the white disc set 156 opposite the hour index on the black scale. On the outer black scale opposite 486 on the white scale read 187 minutes (or 3 hours and 7 minutes on the inner black scale).

Example 5.

Known: Time and speed.
Required: Distance.
A pilot wants to know what distance he will travel in 28 minutes traveling at a ground speed of 148 miles per hour.

SOLUTION: Opposite the hour index on the black dial set 148, on the white dial. Opposite 28 on the black dial read 69 miles on the white dial. (Note: It is not necessary to reset the computer after having once determined speed.)

Thus, in Example 5 above, the pilot may determine the distance traveled in 46 minutes without changing the setting and by merely looking opposite 46 on the black dial for the distance 113 ½ miles on the white dial.

Navitimer, illustration, continued.

Ernest Borel, cocktail, circa 1960s, automatic, stainless, $95-$195.

Breitling Geneve Navitimer, chronograph, circa 1960s, black dial, white bezel, $1,200-$1,600.

Breitling, Navitimer model 806, circa 1967, three register, stainless, $1,000 to $1,800.

Bulova

Highly successful American watch company noted for its Art Deco wrist watches of the 1920s and 1930s, and for the huge success of its "Accutron" tuning-fork watch, produced well into the 1970s.

Bulova, ladies, circa 1920s, unusual 19kt engraved case, engraved sterling silver dial, $100-$250.

Bulova, circa 1920s, chrome stepped case, radium hands with sub-seconds, $75-$175.

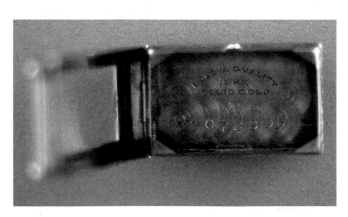

Bulova case, stamped 19kt.

Bulova case back.

A small Bulova watch movement.

Bulova, circa 1930s, chrome tank case engraved bezel, sub-seconds, $95-$195.

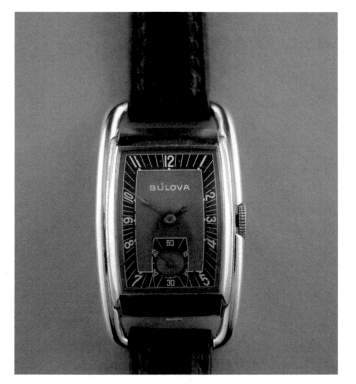

Bulova, circa 1939, gold filled, unusual case, two tone black and gray dial, $200-$400.

Bulova, back dated 1939.

Bulova, ladies, circa 1940s, 14kt WG with diamonds, $195-$395.

Bulova, ladies, circa 1940s, 14kt WG, diamond bracelet, $1,000-$1,750.

Bulova, circa 1940s, diamonds, 23J, 14kt WG, $195-$395.

Bulova, circa 1940s, rose gold dial and case, GF with fancy lugs, $200-$450.

Bulova, 21J movement, pink gold, pink dial, $100-$250.

Bulova, circa 1950s, WGF case, hidden lugs, $75-$175.

Restored Bulova, circa 1950s, gold filled diamond dial, after dial restoration, $95-$195.

Bulova, circa 1950s, raised gold markers, $75-$150.

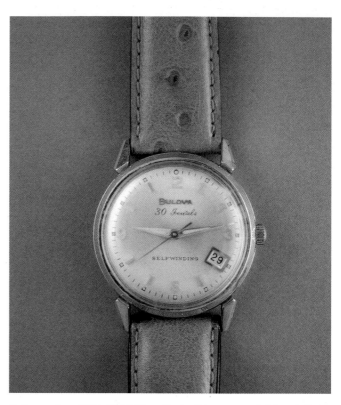

Bulova, circa 1966, GF, 30J, self winding, unusual date window at 4:00, $100-$250.

Bulova, Accutron 214, circa 1966 (M6), GF, $175-$275.

Bulova, Accutron 214, circa 1967 (M7), stainless/unusual lugs, $200-$400.

Bulova Spaceview, Accutron model 214, circa 1971, see through crystal case, stainless, $250-$395.

Bulova, digital LED, 1970s, gold tone, $150-$300.

Bulova, Accutron model 218, circa 1973, stainless, $125-$225.

Bulova, Accutron model 214, circa 1974, railroad approved, $395-$495.

Bulova 214, Accutron Anniversary Edition, gold-plate case, stainless back, designed in the shape of the Accutron tuning fork, Spaceview, $395-$595.

Bulova Accutron, 214 model back set.

Concord, circa 1940s, platinum and diamond, rose gold, ladies retro watch, $2,500-$3,500.

Corum, peacock feather, circa 1970s, 18kt tank style, $800-$1,000.

Swiss Croton, circa 1960s, sweep seconds, stainless, $75-$175.

Cyma, Tavannes 7J movement, circa WW I, nickel case-grill guard, $195-$395.

Cyma, circa 1920s, sterling flip top push button, radium enamel dial, $495-$795.

Cyma, with top closed.

Elgin, engraved bezel style/base metal, circa 1910s, enamel dial blue spade hands, 15J, $95-$195.

Elgin, 15J movement.

Ebel, ladies Swiss, circa 1960s, 14kt with mesh band, $425-$625.

Montgomery Bros., circa 1911, Elgin 15J movement, sterling-enamel dial, $195-$495.

Elgin, circa 1915, 15J, chrome engraved, radium hands and numerals, $95-$195.

Elgin, military, circa 1917, nickel case, 7J, heavy wire lugs-radium hands, $150-$450.

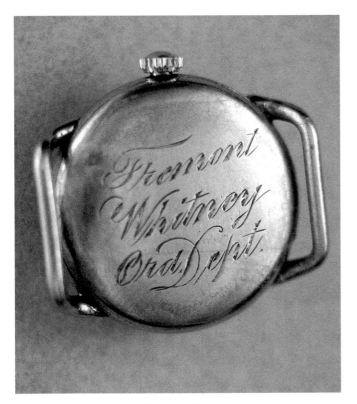

Elgin, engraved on back (Fremont Whitney Ord. Dept.).

Elgin, circa 1918, enamel dial, silver, wire lug, $150-$350.

Elgin, circa 1920s?, 7J, GF, rare case style, $150-$300.

Elgin, circa 1918, 7J, watch band pins riveted on, GF, $100-$250.

Elgin movement.

Elgin, circa 1920s, 7J, enamel dial with sub seconds, GF swivel lugs, $95-$195.

Elgin, circa 1922, 15J, WGF case, engraved bezel edge, $95-$195.

Elgin, circa 1927, 14kt WG barrel-shaped case, large crown, 15J, $75-$150.

Elgin, circa 1929, 7J, WGF case, engraved bezel, $75-$175.

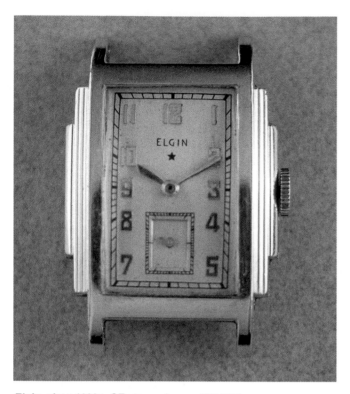

Elgin, circa 1930s, GF stepped case, $95-$225.

ELGIN WRIST WATCHES FOR MEN

Attractive Popular Models Offering Unusual Values.

Truly fine timepieces of guaranteed quality. Complete factory products, cased, timed and regulated at the Elgin factory. Illustrations ⅝ actual size. Handsome gift boxes.
Prices Subject to Wholesale Discounts. See Page 2.

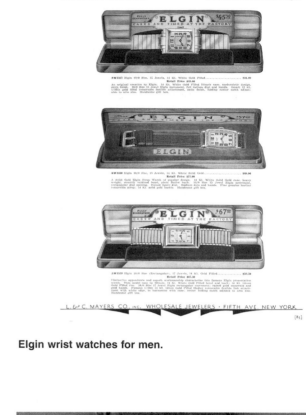

L. & C. MAYERS CO. INC., WHOLESALE JEWELERS · FIFTH AVE, NEW YORK

Elgin wrist watches for men.

ELGIN WRIST WATCHES FOR MEN

Attractive Popular Models Offering Unusual Values.

Truly fine timepieces of guaranteed quality. Complete factory products, cased, timed and regulated at the Elgin plant. Illustrations ⅝ actual size. Handsome gift boxes.
Prices Subject to Wholesale Discounts. See Page 2.

L. & C. MAYERS CO. INC., WHOLESALE JEWELERS · FIFTH AVE, NEW YORK

Elgin wrist watches for men.

Elgin, Avigo, circa 1930s, 7J, chrome case, $100-$250.

Elgin, circa 1932, 7J, WGF engraved square case, $100-$250.

Elgin, circa 1933, curved case, hidden lugs, 7J, chrome case unusual design, $100-$300.

Elgin, mid-size, circa 1939, 15J, sweep second hand, $75-$150.

Elgin-movement and inside case back.

Lord Elgin, driver's style black dial, circa 1950s, 21J, GF, $100-$250.

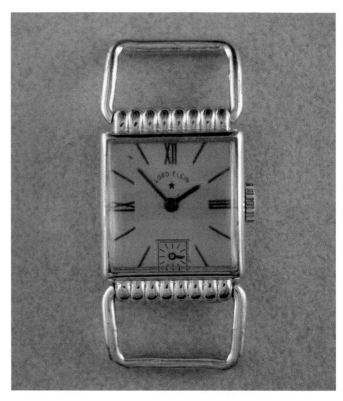

Elgin, driver's watch, pink dial, circa 1950s, 21J, pink GF, $100-$250.

Lord Elgin, circa 1951, 21J, GF, $75-$175.

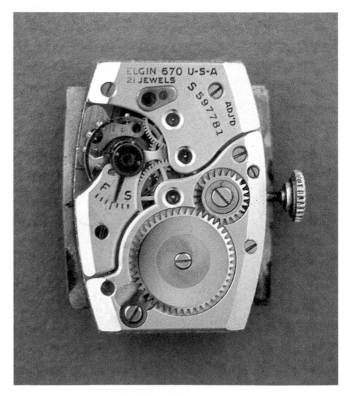

Lord Elgin, movement caliber 670.

Lord Elgin, circa 1950s, gold filled, fancy hidden lugs, $95-$195.

Lord Elgin, circa 1950s, 21J, GF square case, $95-$195.

Elgin, circa 1950s, numerals on bezel, pinwheel dial, GF, $95-$195.

Elgin, circa 1952, 17J, GF, $75-$175.

Elgin, Lord Elgin digital, circa 1950s, 21J caliber movement, GF, $400-$800.

Lord Elgin, circa 1950s, direct read-with box, GF, $495-$695.

Elgin, money clip in box.

Elgin, money clip, circa 1950s, 17J, GF, $95-$295.

Eska, circa 1941, mid-size early self-winding, stainless, radium hands sweep second, $150-$250.

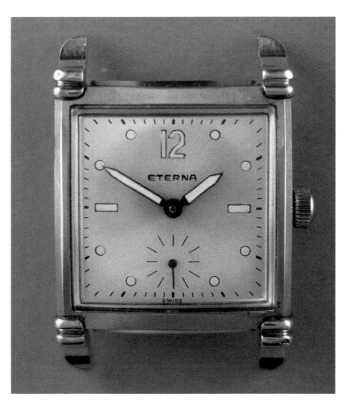

Eterna, restored, circa 1940s, two-tone SS with gold lugs, $195-$495.

Favre Leuba, alarm, circa 1960s, seabird, stainless, $250-$450.

Gelbros Swiss, circa 1920s, fancy engraved chrome case, radium hands, $100-$200.

Girard-Perregaux, Switzerland

Founded in the 1850s, this company is known to have been the first to produce wrist watches (1880s) for military use.

Girard Perregaux, Gyromatic, chrome plated, 17J, $95-$195.

Girard Perregaux, Gyromatic, circa late 1950s-1960s, SS back/gold top/original dial, screw back, $100-$250.

Gruen Watch Co., Cincinnati, Ohio

Founded in the 1870s in Columbus, Ohio, Gruen is famous for its imported Swiss "Guild" movements, and for the "Veri-Thin," "Curvex," and "Doctors" watches.

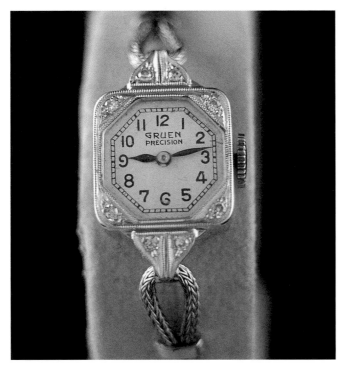

Gruen Precision, ladies, circa 1920s, 14kt WG, diamond, $395-$795.

Gruen, circa 1930s, 17J, GF barrel shape, $95-$195.

Gruen Swiss, circa 1930, 15J, GF stepped case, $95-$195.

Gruen, Veri-Thin, circa 1940s, 24-hour military dial radium hands, GF, $100-$250.

Gruen, ladies curvex, circa 1930s, GF, $100-$250.

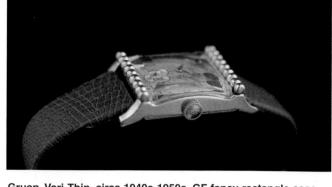

Gruen, Veri-Thin, circa 1940s-1950s, GF fancy rectangle case, $100-$250.

Gruen, Precision, circa 1950s, auto wind/sweep second, GF, $75-$175.

Gruen, Precision, auto-wind, circa 1960s, day-date, SS, $75-$175.

Gubelin, circa 1940s, restored/refinished dial, SS, original hands, $100-$300.

Hamilton Watch Co.

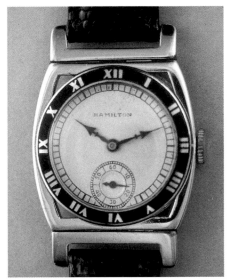

Hamilton, square, circa 1923, green GF-enameled bezel, sub-seconds at 9:00, rare.

Hamilton, Piping Rock, circa 1928, 14kt white or yellow, enamel bezel, $800-$1,400.

Hamilton "Dixon," circa 1936, stepped lugs, applied numerals, 17J 987E movement, GF, $100-$250.

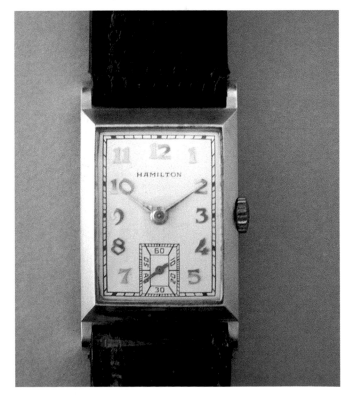

Hamilton Seckron, circa 1936, GF, doctor's watch, $800-$1,300.

Hamilton Rutledge, circa 1936, platinum, $1,200-$2,500.

Hamilton, Dodson, circa 1937, 17J, GF, $100-$275.

Hamilton Gilman, circa 1937, 14kt, $350-$700.

Hamilton Sidney, circa 1937, GF, $100-$300.

Hamilton, circa 1930s, 17J 986 caliber, rare sub seconds at 9:00, GF/early refinished dial, $200-$300.

Hamilton, circa 1930s, 987A movement, barrel shape, 17J, $100-$200.

Hamilton, Coronado, circa 1930s, 14kt WG swivel lugs, black enamel bezel, $1,000-$2,400.

Hamilton Coronado, photo on roses.

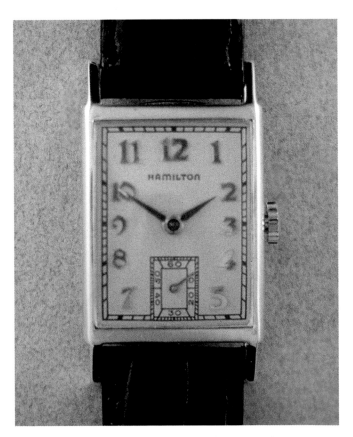

Hamilton "Brock," circa 1939, Grade 982, 14kt, 19J, $395-$795.

32

★ HAMILTON WATCH ★

★ Grade 979—Hamilton Strap Watches—Grade 987 ★

Glenn Curtiss
An aristocratic model, designed with a fine sense of proportion. In handmade case of 14K yellow or white gold. Consumer price, $150.00.

Coronado
A distinctly different, ultra-modern strap watch of unusual beauty and accuracy. Available in 14K yellow or white gold. Consumer price, $125.00.

Captain Rice
Extreme simplicity of design distinguishes this strap watch by Hamilton. In handmade case of 14K white and yellow gold. Consumer price, $150.00.

Piping Rock
An exceedingly smart and masculine strap watch styled by designers of international prominence. In 14K yellow or white gold. Consumer price, $125.00.

Cambridge
A distinctive sports watch by Hamilton, altogether modern in treatment and design. Available in 14K yellow or white gold. Consumer price, $125.00.

Meadowbrook
In 14K yellow or white gold. Consumer price, $100.00. Also available in platinum case with white gold buckle. Consumer price, $360.00. With platinum buckle, consumer price, $400.00.

Unprecedented consumer acceptance, and an increasing demand for greater variety in case designs, have made necessary the addition of four new models to this Hamilton Grade 979.

Regarded as an exclusive watch by those who are satisfied only with the best, each member is a 19-jewel Hamilton of unusual accuracy. These 6/0 size watches are temperature adjusted, with highly polished ratchet and winding wheel, and extra fine flute damaskeening.

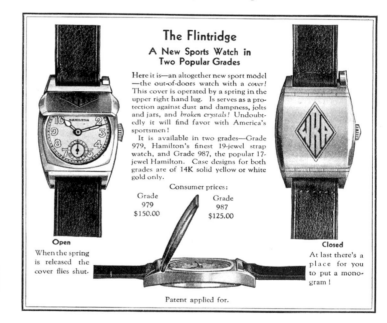

The Flintridge
A New Sports Watch in Two Popular Grades

Here it is—an altogether new sport model—the out-of-doors watch with a *cover!* This cover is operated by a spring in the upper right hand lug. Is serves as a protection against dust and dampness, jolts and jars, and *broken crystals!* Undoubtedly it will find favor with America's sportsmen!

It is available in two grades—Grade 979, Hamilton's finest 19-jewel strap watch, and Grade 987, the popular 17-jewel Hamilton. Case designs for both grades are of 14K solid yellow or white gold only.

Consumer prices:

Grade 979 $150.00   Grade 987 $125.00

Open
When the spring is released the cover flies shut.

Closed
At last there's a place for you to put a monogram!

Patent applied for.

Hamilton Grade 987 Strap Watches in Solid Gold

Langley
A distinguished 17-jewel Hamilton for the man of to-day. Available in 14K solid yellow or white gold only. Consumer price $90.00.

Pinehurst
A smartly engraved strap watch of 14K yellow or white gold only. Raised gold figure dial No. 047 or regular luminous dial at no extra charge. Consumer price, $90.00.

Hastings
For the sportsman—a sturdy 17-jewel strap watch in 14K solid yellow or white gold. Consumer price, $85.00. Also available in 14K filled gold, yellow or white. Consumer price, $55.00.

Hamilton

The Watch of Railroad Accuracy

Consumers' Prices Only on This Page—For List Prices See Page 35

Early Hamilton wrist watch ad.

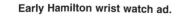

Hamilton, circa 1940s, WGF, 17J 752 movement, applied numerals, $100-$250.

Hamilton "Martin," circa 1941, 987A movement, GF, $100-$200.

Hamilton, military WW II, new-old stock, $300-$400.

Hamilton, military WW II, back of case.

Hamilton "Secometer," circa 1946, 987S movement, sweep second, GF, $75-$175.

Hamilton "Roland," circa 1946, GF ribbed case, $195-$395.

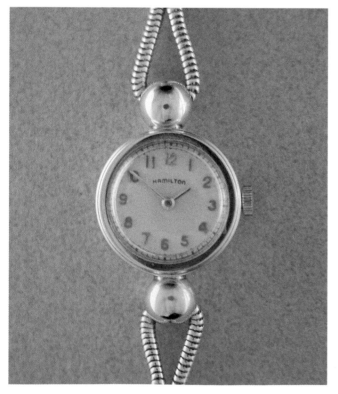

Hamilton, ladies, circa 1940s, 14kt case/round balls at lug, $150-$250.

Hamilton, circa 1948, 17J 747 movement, GF square, $100-$200.

Hamilton, contract case, produced in various precious metals, late 1940s, diamond dial, $600-$2,000.

Hamilton, circa 1950s, GF, applied numerals, auto wind/power indicator, $150-$250.

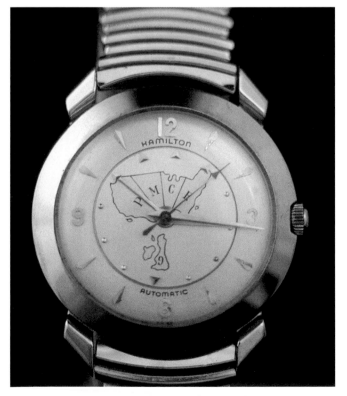

Hamilton, Transcontinental A, circa 1955, GF/time-zone dial, $300-$750.

Hamilton, Spectra Electric, circa 1957, 18kt, very unusual Hamilton logo dial, $650-$950.

Hamilton, Victor Electric, circa 1957, GF, $125-$375.

Hamilton, Van Horn Electric, circa 1957, 14kt, $300-$500.

Hamilton, Ventura Electric, circa 1957, 14kt yellow, $1,200-$1,800.

Hamilton, Ventura Electric, circa 1958, 14kt white diamond dial, $3,000-$5,000.

Hamilton, Ventura Electric, late 1950s, 18kt pink gold, very rare.

Hamilton "Titan," electric, circa 1958, GF stepped case, $150-$300.

Hamilton, Everest Electric, circa 1958, GF, $200-$500.

Hamilton, Converta II Electric, circa 1958, SS/14kt bezel, $250-$500.

Hamilton, Vantage Electric, circa 1958, GF, $100-$350.

Hamilton "Prentice," circa 1959, RGF, author's gold and rosewood band attached, $95-$195.

Hamilton, Regulus Electric, circa 1959, SS, $300-$800.

Hamilton "Thin-O-Matic" (rare), automatic, circa 1960, two-tone dial, GF, $395-$695.

Hamilton, Saturn Electric, circa 1960, GF, $200-$500.

Hamilton, Sherwood S, circa 1961, GF with teak dial and band inserts, unusual.

Hamilton, Altair Electric, circa 1962, GF, original band, $1,800-$3,000.

Hamilton, Pacer Electric, circa 1958, GF, $250-$750.

Hamilton, Pacer Electric, circa late 1950s, corporate logo dial, $300-$700.

Hamilton Pacermatic (automatic movement), circa 1961, GF/rare, beware of fakes.

Hamilton, Savitar Electric, circa 1962, 14kt, $350-$750.

Hamilton, RR special electric, circa 1963, 505 model, stainless, $175-$275.

Hamilton Electric Savitar II, GF, circa 1965, with company logo, $150-$400.

Hamilton Electric Taurus, circa 1962, GF, $100-$300.

Hamilton, Vega Electric, circa 1962, original band, GF, $800-$1,500.

Hamilton, Victor II Electric, circa 1962, GF, original band, $200-$500.

Hamilton, K-475 Automatic, circa 1962, GF, extremely rare, $2,000-$4,000.

Hamilton, Polaris Electric, circa 1963, 14kt, $295-$495.

Hamilton, T-403 Automatic, two-tone dial with date, circa 1965, GF, $395-$695.

Hamilton, Lord Lancaster J Electric, circa 1965, GF/diamond dial, $300-$700.

Hamilton, Odyssee 2001 Automatic, circa 1969, date at 6:00, SS, $500-$900.

Hamilton Vesta, ladies version of the Altair, original box, GF, $300-$700.

Ingersoll, circa 1920s, base metal, inexpensive early wrist watch, $50-$100.

Hilton, circa 1950s, stainless, 17J-manual wind, $75-$150.

Helbros, circa 1950s, 14kt case, diamond dial at 12, 3, and 9, 17J, $125-$275.

Ingraham USA (2), circa 1940s, original crystal yellowed with age, 0 jewel, $25-$75 each.

Illinois Watch Co., Springfield, circa 1918, sterling, 15J, $495-$795.

Illinois Watch Co., movement view.

Illinois, 21J strap watches of character.

Illinois, rectangular strap watches.

The Home of FAITH *Products*   **21**

THE ILLINOIS WATCH

Sturdy 3-0 Size, 17 Jewel Strap Watches

These Illinois watches have proven their worth through many years of service. Thousands of these exceptional watches have checked the hours for men in all walks of life—in all parts of the United States and on the battlefields of France. The 3/0 size movement was used extensively by the United States Government during the late war. Each Illinois 3/0 is thoroughly dependable, and has masculine appeal.

❖   ❖   ❖

The SKYWAY

For Air-Minded America. Designed to meet the particular requirements of aviation, this strapwatch is proving popular throughout the nation. In its makeup you will find no compromise with ordinary watch construction. Equipped with standard aeronautical dial, dust-proof case with screw back and bezel, 14K white gold filled case; extra strength crystal.
Suggested consumer price, $45.

The CHIEFTAIN

6/0 SIZE—15 JEWELS

A fine Illinois Watch at an extremely low price. The engraving design of the Chieftain has been patterned after the signs and symbols of America's first people, giving the watch background an attractive design. The 15 jewel movement is a high grade, accurate example of watchmaking. 14K white and natural filled gold.
Suggested consumer price, $40.

The GUARDSMAN

The Guardsman rotor-dial strapwatch is an unusual idea in men's wrist watches. The rotor-dial provides accurate timing of seconds—and has many advantages. In 14K white and green filled gold, plain or oxidized cases.
Suggested consumer price, $45.

The MATE

A watch for the man of action who demands accuracy under all conditions. The mate is a compact watch of unusual design which affords it extra protection. 14K white or green filled gold; plain or engraved cases.
Suggested consumer price, $42.50.

❖

THE 3/0 SIZE WATCH

The 17 jewel 3/0 size Illinois watch will bear the closest examination. Note the sturdiness of its construction—the 17 Ruby and Sapphire jewels; the compensating balance with its timing screws; the steel escape wheel and the Breguet hairspring; the micrometric screw regulator. Here is a splendid watch which responds to the need for accurate time under severe tests.

The VIKING

An attractive Illinois strapwatch—cased so exceptionally small that it appears more the size of a 6/0 watch. 14K white or natural filled gold.
Suggested consumer price, $42.50.

The SPEEDWAY

A thoroughbred Illinois Watch of craftsmanship. It is a dressy, dependable and sturdy timepiece. This is the watch that withstood the strain of the 1929 Indianapolis race, strapped to the wrists of ten of the leading drivers. 14K white filled gold.
Suggested consumer price, $42.50.

The JOLLY ROGER

A sturdy strapwatch of gay, unconventional design—with an appeal to the adventurous spirit. 14K white and green filled gold— plain, engraved or oxidized cases.
Suggested consumer price, $42.50.

A GREAT AMERICAN WATCH SINCE 1870

Consumers' Prices Only on This Page—For List Prices See Page 27

Illinois, sturdy 3-0 size.

Jaeger-LeCoultre, Switzerland

This fine company dates back to 1833 when Antoine LeCoultre established his watchmaking workshop in Le Sentier, Switzerland. In 1847, LeCoultre produced its first movement with a crown winding and setting system, eliminating the need for watch keys. In 1903, the company unveiled the world's flattest pocket watch caliber, and at 1.38 mm thick, it remains an unbroken record.

In 1925, tiny Art Deco watches were created, featuring the twin-level rectangular Duoplan movement, that were way ahead of their time in terms of accurate timekeeping. In 1929, LeCoultre reduced the mechanical watch movement to its smallest dimension ever—caliber 101. Measuring 14 x 4.8 x 3.4 mm, comprising 98 parts, and weighing around one gram, it is still the world's smallest mechanical movement and is still in production.

In 1931, the company met the challenge to build a watch rugged enough to be worn in sporting events by inventing the Reverso. This wrist watch, with a swivel case, turns its back on shocks to protect the fragile glass. It is one of the few remaining authentic Art Deco creations still being produced. In 1953, Jaeger-LeCoultre developed the Futurematic. This watch is equipped with a power-reserve indicator and is the first automatic watch to require no winding crown. In 1956, the first automatic alarm wrist watch was created, the Memovox. The company still makes fabulous mechanical watches to this day in Le Sentier. The following photos are courtesy of Jaeger-LeCoultre.

Drivers' style watches, with crown at 6 o' clock.

Queen Elizabeth II wore the Jaeger-LeCoultre calibre 101 on her coronation day.

The Duoplan, circa 1925, with a split-level movement.

The first Reverso, circa 1931, the legendary swivel watch.

A 1930's ad for ladies' Reverso.

Day-date models, first made in the 1940s.

Jaeger-LeCoultre Memovox, circa 1956, the first automatic wrist-watch alarm.

Longines, Switzerland

Founded in 1867, Longines became the world's first watch trademark and the first Swiss company to assemble watches under one roof. In 1877, Longines won the first of its 10 World's Fair grand prizes and 28 gold medals, and it was the beginning of Longines' rightful claim to the title of "The World's Most Honored Watch." In 1899, the Duke of Abbruzi completed a successful Arctic Ocean expedition with Longines chronometers used as instrumentation. In 1927, Colonel Charles Lindbergh completed a first non-stop flight from New York to Paris using a Longines watch for time and instrumentation. From 1928 through 1938, the likes of Admiral Byrd, Amelia Earhart, Howard Hughs, Von Schiller, captain of the "Graf Zeppelin," and other adventurers placed their trust in Longines watches. In 1953, Longines developed the first quartz movement. Stainless steel automatics from the 1950s and 1960s are highly collectible, as are the early Longines wrist watches from the 1910s and 1920s.

A 1934 metal toy truck, pictured with the author's 1912 Longines wrist watch.

Longines, circa 1912, enamel dial/Roman numerals, sterling wire lug case, 15J, $195-$395.

Longines, circa 1920s, sterling with solid lugs, enamel dial, $150-$350.

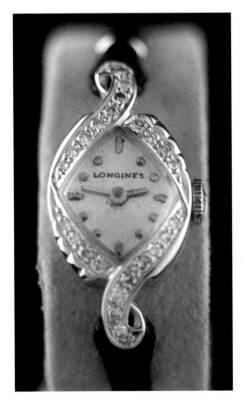

Longines, ladies, circa 1940s, 14kt WG, fancy diamond case, $495-$795.

Longines, circa 1949, 14kt gold, manual wind, $195-$595.

Longines, circa 1952, 17J, GF, $100-$250.

Circa 1937, bracelet band and case set with diamonds, silvered dial with Arabic numerals, square hour markers. Photo courtesy Longines Museum Collection.

Circa 1912, 14kt white gold case set with diamonds, 12 painted Breguet style numerals, external minute track. Photo courtesy Longines Museum Collection.

Circa 1919 "Tonneau" style, enamel dial/Breguet style numerals, silver/935. Photo courtesy Longines Museum Collection.

Circa 1937, stainless steel, silvered dial with Arabic numerals, sub-dial for seconds at the 6. Photo courtesy Longines Museum Collection.

Circa 1972, 900/silver, ladies-men's wristwatches manual wind, the Serge Manzon Collection. Photo courtesy Longines Museum Collection.

Marvin Watch Co.-Swiss, circa 1942, radium hands sub seconds, base metal, mirror effect on dial, $50-$125.

Mido, multifort automatic, circa 1940s, stainless, mid-size, $75-$175.

Mido, multifort, circa 1950s, super automatic power wind, stainless, $75-$175.

Movado, circa 1914, white gold half moon-shaped case. Photo courtesy of Movado Watch Co.

Movado, close up of the Chronograph's 17J Swiss movement.

H.Y. Moser &Cie, oversized/conversion/pocket watch to wrist watch, circa 1910s, $295-$595.

Movado, ladies, circa 1960s, 14kt gold with mesh band, extra small, $695-$895.

Ulysse Nardin, vintage wrist repeater, est. $25,000-$40,000.

Moser Longines Omega, large oversized pocket watches converted to wrist watches, circa 1910s, $295-$595.

Moser Longines Omega, all three movements of watches pictured above.

Nehi, New Haven-Tip-Top, circa 1929, chrome, advertising watch, $45-$95.

Nivada Grenchen, Antarctic automatic, circa 1950s, stainless, $195-$395.

Early cushion-shaped Movado lady's watch, in 18kt, made in 1915. Photo courtesy of Movado Watch Co.

Omega, Switzerland

This prolific company first started producing watches in 1848 and is famed for its timing of the Olympics for decades. In 1969, Neil Armstrong stepped onto the lunar surface wearing an Omega Speedmaster Professional, the only watch ever worn on the moon, and to this day the only watch issued to every NASA astronaut. Omega watches are very collectible, especially the "Seamaster" and the "Constellation" automatic models, as well as any of its Chronographs.

Omega (very rare), minute repeater, circa 1892. Photo courtesy of Omega.

Omega, chronograph shown with movement, circa 1913, wire lug case. Photo courtesy of Omega.

Omega, half hunter-demi-hunter, circa 1899, double-pointed hour hand-two dials, $1,500-$2,500.

Omega, military, circa 1916, steel case with protective grill, caliber 13 movement, $295-$595.

Omega chronograph caliber 39, circa 1929, gold button at 6, $3,000-$5,000.

Omega, chronograph, circa 1932, stainless, $2,000-$4,000.

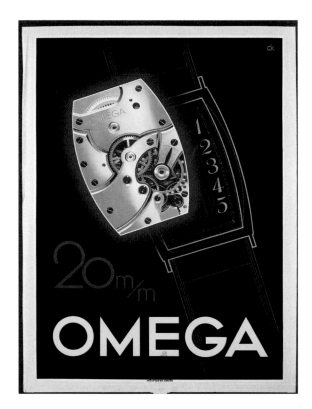

This Omega Art Deco ad dedicated the arrival of the caliber 20 that was launched in 1929.

Omega, circa 1936, 15J-manual wind, black dial roman numerals, $195-$395.

Omega, chronograph military, circa 1937, stainless, $1,500-$2,500.

Omega, left: stainless steel Chronograph, circa 1940; right: wire lug Chronograph, circa 1924. Photo courtesy of Omega.

Omega, Chronometer, circa 1940s, pink gold, rare, $900-$1,800.

Omega, British watch ad, featuring the caliber 30.

Omega, military-RAF (Royal Air Force), circa 1950s, stainless, black dial, $250-$750.

Omega-Aero, oversized, 1950s airplane sub-seconds at 9, two-tone gold with black dial, base metal-pocket watch movement, $250-$500.

Omega, early 1950 automatic-wind movement, caliber 455.

Omega, Ranchero, circa 1958, rare, stainless, ultra anti-magnetic, $1,500-$2,500.

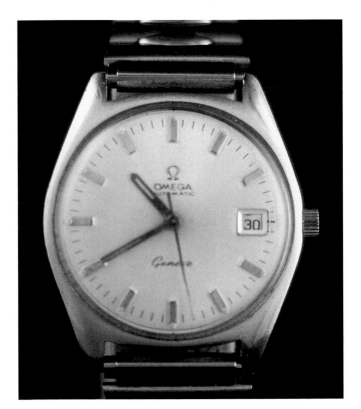

Omega, Geneve, circa 1960s, automatic date, stainless, $125-$275.

Omega Early Speedmaster, Chronograph, circa 1957, stainless with black dial, $1,500-$2,500.

Omega, Speedmaster Professional, three register chronograph, circa 1966, 17J stainless, $1,000-$1,5000.

Omega, Speedmaster Professional, Chronograph, approved by NASA, stainless, $900-$1,400.

Omega, Seamaster DeVille, circa 1960s, stainless and gold two tone, 24J, $300-$600.

Omega Seamaster, circa 1973, stainless, in box.

Omega, circa 1973, Seamaster DeVille stainless, SS Omega band, $250-$500.

Omega, SS clasp and band.

Patek Philippe (rare model), circa 1950s, 18kt rose gold with pink dial, sculptured lugs, indirect sweep seconds, $9,000-$11,000.

Patek Philippe, movement and inside case back.

Omega, pair of Seamaster DeVilles.

Omega, Seamaster DeVille case back.

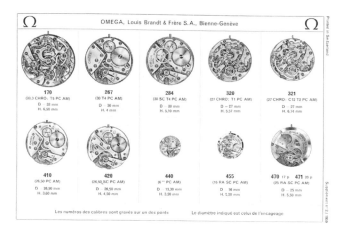

Some more Omega wrist-watch movements.

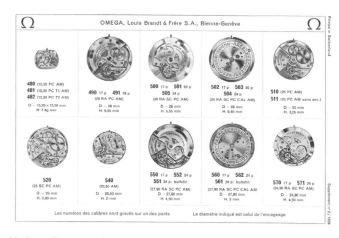

Various Omega wrist-watch movements.

Pulsar LED case back.

Pulsar LED, Time Computer Inc. USA, circa 1970s, GF, $100-$300.

Patek Philippe, contract case 18kt, converted pendant to wrist watch, dial refinished, $2,500.

Philippe Calatrava (rare), original dial-manual wind, circa 1955, stainless-WP case, $7,000-$12,000.

Patek Philippe, Top Hat, circa mid-1940s, original condition, 18kt, $5,000-$7,000.

Patek Philippe, Geneve-Beyer, circa 1970s, stainless WP case, manual wind, $3,500-$4,500.

Pierce, Swiss, 17J Parashock, GF-stainless back, $95-$195.

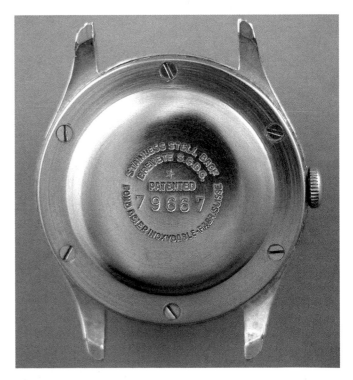

Pierce, note screw-on back.

Rolex, Switzerland

When Rolex started producing the first truly waterproof watch, the "Rolex Oyster," in the later half of the 1920s, it has forever since been associated with high quality and durability. Watch collector connoisseurs love their Rolex, for they know that long after the price is forgotten, the quality remains.

Rolex, circa 1920s, mid-size sterling silver case, 15J, blue enamel bezel, $1,500-$2,000.

Rolex, Viceroy, circa 1930s, stainless case with pink bezel, manual wind, $1,200-$2,400.

Rolex, Oyster Bubble Back, circa 1940s, silver California dial, stainless, $2,000-$4,000.

Rolex, Oyster Raleigh, Ref. #2784, circa 1940s, stainless, $500-$700.

Rolex, Datejust, circa 1950, rare alternate red and black date, 18kt pink gold case with black dial, $3,500-$5,500.

Rolex, Datejust, circa 1953, 14kt gold and stainless case, alternate red/black date, $2,000-$2,500.

Rolex, ref. #6234, Chronograph 72A, circa 1950s, rare, stainless-original dial, $11,000-$14,000.

Rolex, ref. #6234, Chronograph, circa 1950s, 14kt gold case, luminous markers and hands, $18,000-$20,000.

Rolex Oyster Perpetual, ref. #6536, submariner (earliest sub), circa 1950s, indicator on rotating bezel missing, $3,000-$4,000.

Rolex Explorer, ref. #1016, circa 1950s, stainless, $3,000-$4,000.

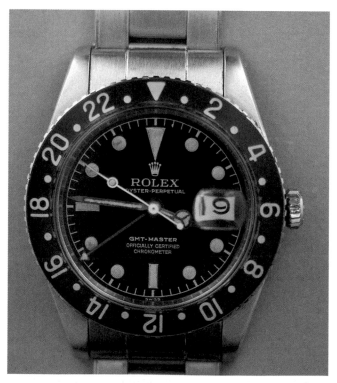

Rolex, GMT Master ref #6542, circa 1955, blue and red bezel, stainless, $2,500-$5,000.

Rolex Oyster Perpetual, ref. #6565, circa 1955, stainless, $1,750-$2,250.

Rolex Tudor, Oyster Prince, circa late 1950s/1960s, self-winding, stainless, $295-$495.

Rolex Oyster Perpetual, ref. #5512, Submariner, circa 1960s, stainless, $2,500-$3,500.

Rolex Oyster Perpetual, GMT Master, ref. #1675, circa 1968, stainless, $2,000-$3,000.

Rolex Oyster Precision, circa 1970, stainless case with pink dial, $1,000-$1,450.

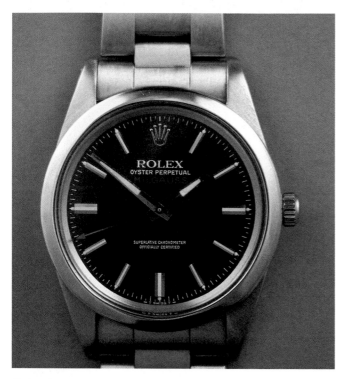

Rolex Oyster Perpetual, Milgauss Chronometer, circa 1970s, stainless-ref. #1019, ultra anti-magnetic, $9,000-$12,000.

Rolex Oyster Cosmograph, Daytona, ref. #6263, circa 1970s, stainless, $9,000-$12,000.

Rolex Oyster Perpetual, Explorer II, ref. #1655, circa mid-1970s, stainless, $4,500-$6,000.

Rolex Explorer Chronometer, ref. #1016, circa 1970s, rare hacking feature, stainless, $3,500-$5,000.

Rolex, Datejust, circa 1970s, stainless and gold, $1,250-$1,850.

Seiko, circa 1930s, chrome case-Hermetic, screw-down bezel, flip-out watch to wind and set, $900-$1,200.

Seiko, with screw-down bezel removed.

Seiko flip-out case.

Seiko, circa 1920s, small size-very early, wire lug, $195-$295.

Seiko movement view.

Seiko, circa 1930s, 24-hour military style, red hours inner chapter, manual wind case within a case, $395-$595.

Seiko, 24-hour military style, out of case.

Seiko, early automatic, circa 1960s, $200-$300.

Japanese Oversized, rare Air Force watch, original strap, circa late 1930s, brushed chrome, sweep seconds, $3,000-$4,000.

Japanese Air Force watch, original leather strap.

Case back with Japanese inscription.

Seiko Super, circa 1960s, 15J manual wind, stainless, $95-$195.

Seiko Super movement.

Seiko, circa 1960s, mid-size, manual wind, stainless case, $95-$195.

Seiko, Chronograph, stainless case rotating bezel, manual wind, black dial, $150-$300.

Geo C. Shreve and Co., circa 1920 San Francisco, chrome case with large lugs, Swiss movement, enamel dial, $250-$500.

Shreve & Co., circa 1920s, rose gold/wire lugs, $700-$1,000.

Shreve & Co., circa 1940s, Swiss Concord movement, stainless-automatic, $400-$700.

Shreve and Co., International Watch Co. movement, circa 1941, stainless steel/radium dial, $900-$1,200.

Tavannes, circa 1910s, enamel dial with leather protector watch strap, nickel case, $195-$295.

Tavannes, circa 1910s, with leather protector watch strap.

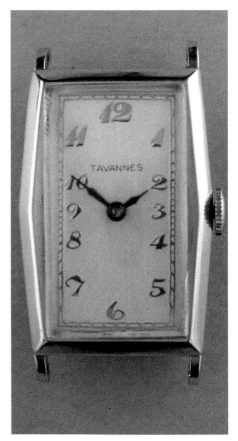

Seiko, circa 1960s, 17J, stainless-faceted crystal, ladies, $50-$150.

Tavannes, Art Deco 1920s, 14kt rose gold massive curved case, gold dial with exploding numerals, made for Russian market, $1,500-$2,000.

Tavannes, circa 1940, WGF, $75-$175.

Tissot, Switzerland

Started in 1853, Charles F. Tissot founded a small watch factory in Le Locle, Switzerland. Tissot supplied watches to Russia and the "Tsar's Court." This fine company merged with the Omega Watch Co. in 1929 and still produces a line of quality watches to the present day. The company has produced many fine wrist watches and pocket watches, including chronometer escapements. The following photos are courtesy of Tissot.

Early Tissot parts box.

Mathey Tissot, circa 1970s, automatic date feature, $75-$150.

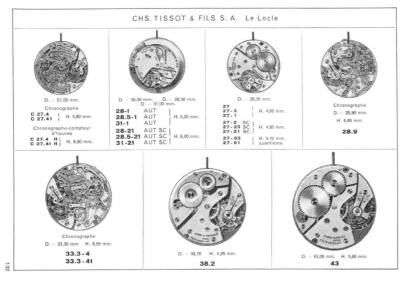

Tissot movements.

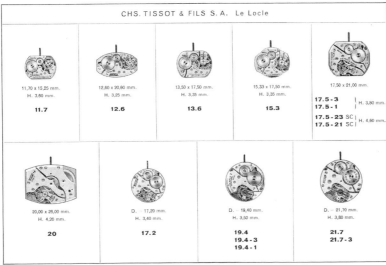

Various Tissot wrist-watch movements.

Tissot, Navigator, circa 1953, world time, automatic, stainless, $1,000-$1,500.

Wakmann, three-register Chronograph, circa 1940s, stainless, $250-$500.

Waltham, circa 1910s, base metal case with metal dial, blue spade hands, 15J, $95-$145.

Waltham, circa 1930, 15J "sapphire" movement, ribbed case near lugs, yellowed crystal, $50-$125.

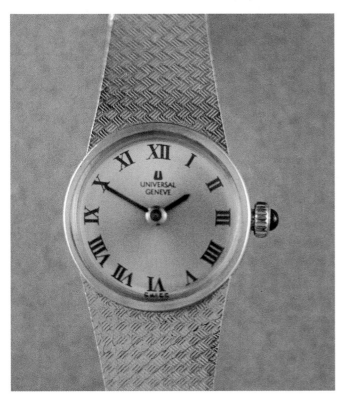

Universal Geneve, ladies, circa 1950s, 14kt gold, $495-$795.

Vulcain, circa 1960s, 17J automatic, stainless, $75-$125.

Waltham, circa 1934, GF, 17J "Ruby" movement, $100-$200.

Waltham, 17J "Ruby" movement.

WALTHAM WRIST WATCHES FOR MEN
The Most Popular Models of This Famous Make

Complete Waltham products; cased, timed and regulated at the factory.   Illustrations ⅞ actual size.   Furnished in handsome gift boxes.   *Prices Subject to Wholesale Discounts.   See Page 2.*

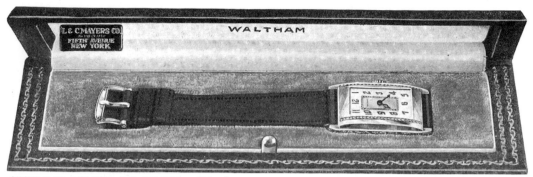

AW1530 14 Kt. Solid White Gold, Full Radium Dial.. $89.00
AW1531 14 Kt. Solid White Gold, Embossed Gold Numerals.. 89.00
Retail Price $90.00

A custom built, thin model 14 Kt. Solid Gold heavy weight case with curved back to fit wrist.   Hand engraved stripes.   Gray satin finish.   Renowned 7¼ ligne 17 Jewel Waltham rectangular adjusted movement.   Fine genuine leather detachable strap; 14 Kt. solid gold buckle.   Elegant gift box.

—Stylish attachments for men's wrist watches shown on page 79.—

AW1532 14 Kt. White Gold, Full Radium Numerals................. $64.00
AW1533 14 Kt. White Gold, Embossed Gold Numerals............... 64.00
Retail Price $65.00

A handsome thin model watch case by Wadsworth.   14 Kt. Solid White Gold, substantial weight.   Plain polished bezel, satin finish, curved back to fit wrist.   Famous 10 ligne 15 Jewel Waltham movement.   Detachable fine genuine leather strap, 14 Kt. solid gold buckle.   Fine gift box.

AW1534 14 Kt. Yellow Gold, 17 Jewels Adjusted..................... $68.00
Retail Price $80.00

An original creation by Wadsworth that has become very popular.   14 Kt. Solid Yellow Gold thin model heavy weight case.   Raised bezel; black enamel numerals.   Satin finish throughout.   6/0 Size, 17 Jewel Waltham adjusted movement.   Detachable fine genuine leather strap, 14 Kt. solid gold buckle.   An unusual timepiece.   Elegant gift box.

AW1535 14 Kt. Yellow Gold, 17 Jewels Adjusted..................... $73.00
AW1536 14 Kt. White Gold, 17 Jewels Adjusted...................... 73.00
Retail Price $80.00

Smart new 14 Kt. Solid Gold heavy weight plain case by Keystone.   Thin model, bright bezel, satin finish back.   6/0 Size, 17 Jewel Waltham adjusted movement; full radium dial as illustrated or embossed gold numerals.   Fine detachable genuine leather strap; 14 Kt. solid gold buckle.   Elegant gift box.   **Specify type of dial when ordering.**

AW1537 14 Kt. Yellow Gold Filled, 15 Jewels........................ $49.50
AW1538 14 Kt. White Gold Filled, 15 Jewels......................... 49.50
Retail Price $50.00

Smart stylish plain thin model 14 Kt. White Gold Filled case by Keystone.   Polished bezel, plain satin back.   Dependable 6/0 Size Waltham 15 Jewel movement, full radium dial.   Gold filled loose link removable attachment harmonizes with case.   Elegant gift box.
Fine genuine leather straps; 1/10th 14 Kt. gold filled buckles furnished for 80c. list additional.

AW1539 14 Kt. White Gold Filled, 15 Jewels......................... $53.50
Retail Price $55.00

Stylish thin model rectangular case by Wadsworth.   14 Kt. White Gold filled, neat satin finish.   Oxidized effect on bezel, satin finish back.   Reliable 10 ligne Waltham 15 Jewel movement, full radium dial and hands.   Smart gold filled removable link attachment harmonizing.   Fine gift box.
Fine genuine leather straps; 1/10th 14 Kt. gold filled buckles furnished for 80c. list additional.

AW1540 14 Kt. White Gold Filled, 7 Jewels.......................... $41.00
Retail Price $42.50

Stylish thin model rectangular case by Wadsworth.   14 Kt. White Gold filled, neat satin finish; Oxidized design on bezel, satin finish back.   Reliable 10 ligne Waltham 7 Jewel movement, full radium dial and hands.   Detachable fine genuine leather strap; buckle same quality as case.   Elegant gift box.

L. & C. MAYERS CO., INC. WHOLESALE JEWELERS · FIFTH AVE. NEW YORK

[85]

Waltham wrist watches for men, from a 1932 catalog.

Waltham, circa 1937, GF, 17J Crescent St. movement, $100-$225.

Waltham, circa 1950, GF-black dial, 25J, $100-$250.

Waltham, Incabloc Swiss, circa late 1950s, GF 17J, sub-seconds, $45-$95.

Wittnauer, circa 1970s, day date/manual wind, unusual blue dial with years, stainless, $175-$275.

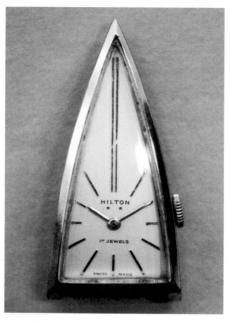

Welsbro, asymmetrical, GF, ladies Swiss, 1950s, $95-$150.

Asymmetrical, circa 1950s ladies Swiss, GF, 17J, $95-$150.

Wittnauer, circa 1940s, sub-seconds automatic, GF, $95-$195.

Wittnauer, ladies, circa 1960s, 14kt case GF band, $100-$200.

Wittnauer, ladies watch movement.

Wyler, Chronograph, circa 1940s, stainless, $395-$795.

Wyler, circa 1940s, stainless-Incaflex, sub-seconds, $95-$195.

Zenith, William Farmer & Co. LTD, Sydney, circa 1920s, Swiss 17J, wire lug, $150-$350.

Zenith movement.

Zodiac, factory box open.

Zodiac, watch box papers and warranty.

Zodiac Sea Wolf, automatic, rotating bezel, stainless, $150-$350.

Miscellaneous Swiss

Swiss, circa 1910s, pin set onion crown, radium black dial, wire lug, $600-$800.

Swiss, circa 1910s, silver wire lug, radium dial and hands, $150-$350.

Swiss, pin set-wire lug, silver and gold engraved case back, enamel dial, $295-$595.

Swiss wire lug case back.

Hansel Sloan and Co., Swiss, circa 1920s, silver/enamel dial, $350-$500.

Hansel Sloan and Co., high-grade Swiss movement.

Swiss, circa 1920s, sterling case with wire lugs, $250-$450.

F. De Ferrari & Co., San Francisco, CA, circa 1920s, sterling enamel dial, roman numerals, $150-$350.

Swiss Chronometer, circa 1920s, sterling silver wire lug case, radium numbers and hands/red military style, $195-$395.

Swiss, Trojan, 17J Swiss Alpina movement, metal radium dial, stainless, $75-$195.

Robert Cart-Swiss, circa 1940s, stainless, $95-$295.

Tian Hadan, signed art watch, circa 1970, manual wind, stainless, $300-$450.

Swiss, ladies, circa 1940, 14kt rose gold case and band, copper dial, $550-$950.

Swiss Rima, bracelet watch, circa 1940s, GF, 1-inch wide engraved band, $95-$195.

Rulon, circa 1940s, .750 total weight diamonds, platinum, fancy bracelet band, $900-$1,250.

Swiss Time Square, circa 1930s, pin-back watch, sterling silver-Helbros movement, rubies-diamonds, $250-$500.

Time Square pin-watch back.

Swiss, mesh flip-top bracelet watch, circa 1960s, 14kt gold w/diamonds, $995-$1,495.

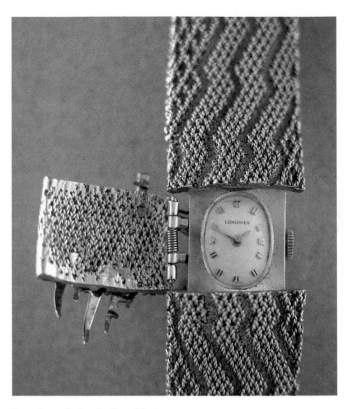

Longines Swiss ladies, flip-top open.

Omega, 1922 Art Deco, case is 18kt gold with floral-enamel design, cathedral hands with engraved bow gilt dial. Photo courtesy of Omega.

Omega, circa 1925 Art Deco, 18kt, enamel cloisonné case. Photo courtesy of Omega.

Patek Philippe pendant watch, circa 1890s, blue enamel and diamond, $3,000-$5,000.

Swiss ladies pendant watch, enamel and gold case, $150-$300.

Swiss pendant watch, circa 1920s, Art Deco, blue, purple, and green enamel, geometric design, $95-$225.

Swiss pendant watch, geometric Art Deco back.

Swiss Ball pendant watch, round enameled, circa 1920s, turquoise enamel gold accents, matching chain, $95-$225.

Pendant watch ornate top.

Pendant watch hanging.

Swiss lapel watch, circa 1920s, sterling with gold wash, blue stones, $95-$195.

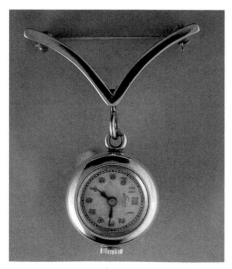

Lapel watch case back.

Fancy enamel cherub and floral watch stand, circa 1880, holds small ladies cylinder watch, $700.

Swiss lapel watch, Acme, circa 1940s, GF, two-tone rose face, $75-$150.

Swiss Acme lapel watch back.

Tradition Swiss, ring watch, manual wind, circa 1960s, $25-$75.

Rhinestone ring watch, Swiss movement, circa 1940s, $35-$95.

Roxhall, wallet watch, Germany, leather, $50-$100.

Cigarette case with watch, circa 1940s, $95-$150.

Character Watches

Swiss Patria lighter/watch, circa 1960s, Gisa Time Lite, 17J, $40-$70.

Ingersoll, character watch, Mickey Mouse, circa 1930s, steel case, original band, paper dial-sub seconds, $250-$750.

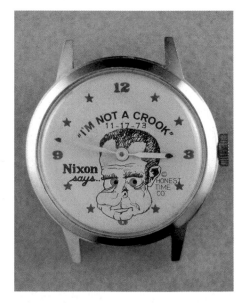

Character watch, Honest Time Co., Nixon, circa 1970s, eyes move side to side as it ticks, $75-$175.

Character watch, U.S. time, circa 1940s, Mickey Mouse, steel case, original red band, $95-$195.

Character watch, Dick Tracy, circa 1940s, stainless, $125-$325.

Character watch, Hopalong Cassidy, U.S. time, steel case, $50-$200.

Hopalong Cassidy watch, back of case engraved "Good Luck from Hoppy."

Hopalong Cassidy, in original box with saddle, steel case, character watch, $495-$595.

Production Numbers and Dates

The following are approximate production numbers and dates of various watch companies (source: American Watchmakers-Clockmakers Institute):

Ansonia

1910	1,000,000
1915	3,000,000
1920	5,000,000
1925	7,000,000
1930	10,000,000

Auburndale

1880	3,000
1885	9,000

Aurora

1885	60,000
1886	110,000
1887	160,000
1888	200,000
1889	215,000

Ball

Made in Elgin, Waltham, Hamilton, and Illinois factories, which accounts for more than one series of numbers.

1900	60,701
420,000	
1905	202,001
462,000	
1910	216,201
600,000	
1915	250,000
603,000	
1920	260,000
610,000	
1925	270,000
1928	800,000
1930	801,000
637,000	
1931	803,000
1935	641,000
1938	647,000
1939	650,000
1940	651,000
1941	652,000
1942	654,000

Bannatyne Watch Co.

1906	40,000
1908	140,000
1910	250,000

Bulova

On the back of many Bulova watchcases are letters and numbers indicating the year of manufacture.

Year	Symbols
1946	46
1947	47
1948	4B
1949	J9
1950	L0
1951	L1
1952	L2
1953	L3
1954	L4
1955	L5
1956	L6
1957	L7
1958	L8
1959	L9
1960	M0
1961	M1
1962	M2
1963	M3
1964	M4
1965	M5
1966	M6
1967	M7
1968	M8
1969	M9
1970	N0
1971	N1
1972	N2
1973	N3
1974	N4

Cheshire

1890	50,000
1895	100,000

Columbus

1883	20,000
1884	50,000
1885	80,000
1886	100,000
1887	130,000
1888	160,000
1889	190,000
1890	225,000
1891	250,000
1892	275,000
1893	300,000
1894	340,000
1895	355,000
1896	380,000
1897	400,000
1898	415,000
1899	435,000
1900	460,000
1901	475,000
1902	485,000
1903	500,000

Dudley Watch Co.

Dudley Watch Co., 1920-1925, 500-2,000
P. W. Baker Co., 1925-1935, 2,001-4,800
XL Watch Co., 1935-1976, 4,801-6,500

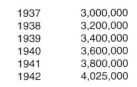

1948	46,000,000
1949	47,000,000
1950	48,000,000
1951	49,000,000
1952	50,000,000

Charles Fasoldt Watch Co.

1855-1864	5-80
1865-1868	90-161
1868-1878	335-540

1937	3,000,000
1938	3,200,000
1939	3,400,000
1940	3,600,000
1941	3,800,000
1942	4,025,000

Elgin

1867	101
1870	100,000
1872	200,000
1874	300,000
1875	400,000
1877	500,000
1879	600,000
1880	700,000
1881	800,000
1882	900,000
1884	1,000,000
1885	1,800,000
1886	2,0000
1888	3,000,000
1890	4,000,000
1893	5,000,000
1895	6,000,000
1897	7,000,000
1899	8,000,000
1900	9,000,000
1903	10,000,000
1904	11,000,000
1905	12,000,000
1907	13,000,000
1909	14,000,000
1910	15,000,000
1911	16,000,000
1912	17,000,000
1914	18,000,000
1916	19,000,000
1917	20,000,000
1918	21,000,000
1919	22,000,000
1920	23,000,000
1921	24,000,000
1922	25,000,000
1923	26,000,000
1924	27,000,000
1925	28,000,000
1926	29,000,000
1927	30,000,000
1928	31,000,000
1929	32,000,000
1930	33,000,000
1933	34,000,000
1934	35,000,000
1936	36,000,000
1938	37,000,000
1939	38,200,000
1940	39,100,000
1941	40,200,000
1942	41,100,000
1943	42,200,000
1945	43,200,000
1947	45,000,000

Hamilton

1893	1,000
1894	5,000
1895	10,000
1896	14,000
1897	20,000
1898	30,000
1899	40,000
1900	50,000
1901	90,000
1902	150,000
1903	260,000
1904	340,000
1905	425,000
1906	590,000
1907	756,000
1908	921,000
1909	1,050,000
1910	1,087,000
1911	1,290,000
1912	1,331,000
1913	1,370,000
1914	1,410,000
1915	1,450,000
1916	1,517,000
1917	1,580,000
1918	1,650,000
1919	1,700,000
1920	1,790,000
1921	1,860,000
1922	1,900,000
1923	1,950,000
1924	2,000,000
1925	2,100,000
1926	2,200,000
1927	2,250,000
1928	2,300,000
1929	2,350,000
1930	2,400,000
1931	2,450,000
1932	2,500,000
1933	2,600,000
1934	2,700,000
1935	2,800,000
1936	2,900,000

Hampden

1875	40,000
1877	60,000
1878	91,000
1879	122,000
1880	153,000
1881	184,000
1882	215,000
1883	250,000
1884	300,000
1885	350,000
1886	400,000
1887	450,000
1888	500,000
1889	555,500
1890	611,000
1891	666,500
1892	722,000
1893	775,000
1894	833,000
1895	888,500
1896	944,000
1897	1,000,000
1898	1,128,000
1899	1,256,000
1900	1,384,000
1901	1,512,000
1902	1,642,000
1903	1,768,000
1904	1,896,000
1905	2,024,000
1906	2,152,000
1907	2,280,000
1908	2,408,000
1909	2,536,000
1910	2,664,000
1911	2,792,000
1912	2,920,000
1913	3,048,000
1914	3,176,000
1915	3,304,000
1916	3,432,000
1917	3,560,000
1918	3,680,000
1919	3,816,000
1920	3,944,000
1921	4,072,000
1922	4,200,000
1923	4,400,000
1924	4,600,000

Howard

1859	20,000
1860	44,000
1870	200,000
1880	550,000
1890	700,000
1900	850,000
1909	980,000
1912	1,100,000
1915	1,285,000
1917	1,340,000
1921	1,400,000
1930	1,500,000

Illinois

1872	First watch made
1873	20,000
1874	50,000
1875	75,000
1876	100,000
1877	125,000
1878	150,000
1879	170,000
1880	200,000
1881	220,000
1882	230,000
1883	250,000
1884	285,000
1885	310,000
1886	340,000
1887	350,000
1888	360,000
1889	380,000
1890	400,000
1891	430,000
1892	460,000
1893	470,000
1894	525,000
1895	590,000
1896	650,000
1897	700,000

1898	850,000
1899	900,000
1900	1,300,000
1902	1,500,000
1903	1,650,000
1904	1,700,000
1905	1,800,000
1906	1,840,000
1907	1,900,000
1908	2,100,000
1909	2,150,000
1910	2,200,000
1911	2,300,000
1912	2,400,000
1913	2,500,000
1914	2,600,000
1915	2,700,000
1916	2,800,000
1917	3,000,000
1918	3,200,000
1919	3,400,000
1920	3,600,000
1921	3,750,000
1922	3,900,000
1923	4,000,000
1924	4,500,000
1925	4,700,000
1926	4,800,000
1927	5,000,000
(Company sold to Hamilton)	
1928	5,200,000
1929	5,350,000
1930	5,400,000
1931	5,500,000
1932	5,600,000

Ingersoll

1892	150,000
1893	310,000
1894	650,000
1895	1,000,000
1896	2,000,000
1897	2,900,000
1898	3,500,000
1899	3,750,000
1900	6,000,000
1901	6,700,000
1902	7,200,000
1903	7,900,000
1904	8,100,000
1905	10,000,000
1906	12,500,000
1907	15,000,000
1908	17,500,000
1909	20,000,000
1910	25,000,000

1911	30,000,000
1912	38,500,000
1913	40,000,000
1914	41,500,000
1915	42,500,000
1916	45,500,000
1917	47,000,000
1918	47,500,000
1919	50,000,000
1920	55,000,000
1921	58,000,000
1922	60,500,000
1923	62,000,000
1924	65,000,000
1925	67,500,000
1926	69,000,000
1927	70,500,000
1928	71,500,000
1929	73,500,000
1930	75,000,000

E. Ingraham

1905	50,000
1910	250,000
1915	2,000,000
1920	4,000,000
1925	7,000,000
1930	10,000,000

Lancaster

1880	50,000
1885	100,000
1890	150,000

A. Lange & Sohne

1870	1,500
1875	10,000
1880	20,000
1885	25,000
1890	30,000
1895	35,000
1900	40,000
1905	50,000
1910	60,000
1915	70,000
1920	75,000
1925	80,000
1930	85,000
1935	90,000
1940	100,000

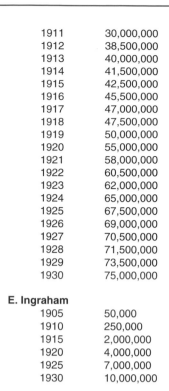

Longines

1867	1
1870	20,000

1880	200,000
1882	250,000
1888	500,000
1890	600,000
1893	750,000
1899	1,000,000
1900	1,200,000
1901	1,250,000
1904	1,500,000
1905	1,750,000
1910	2,000,000
1920	3,000,000
1930	5,000,000
1940	6,000,000

Manhattan
1885	200,000
1895	500,000

Manistee
1910	40,000
1915	60,000

New Haven Clock and Watch Co.
1890	2,000,000
1895	3,000,000
1900	5,000,000
1905	7,000,000
1910	10,000,000
1915	14,000,000
1920	18,000,000
1925	25,000,000
1930	30,000,000

Newark Watch Co.
As Newark Watch Co., 1864-1870, 6,901-12,000
As Cornell Watch Co. (Chicago 1870-1874), 12,001-25,000
As Cornell Watch Co. (San Francisco 1874-1876), 25,001-35,000
Ending as the California Watch Co., Jan. 1876-July 1876.

New York Standard
1890	600,000
1895	900,000
1900	1,200,000
1905	1,500,000
1910	1,800,000
1915	2,100,000
1920	2,400,000
1925	2,700,000
1930	3,000,000

Omega (Courtesy of Omega Watch Co.)
1894	1,000,000
1902	2,000,000
1906	3,000,000
1910	4,000,000
1915	5,000,000
1920	6,000,000
1923	7,000,000
1926	8,000,000
1934	9,000,000
1944	10,000,000
1947	11,000,000
1950	12,000,000
1952	13,000,000
1954	14,000,000
1956	15,000,000
1958	16,000,000
1959	17,000,000
1961	18,000,000
1962	19,000,000
1963	20,000,000
1964	21,000,000
1965	22,000,000
1966	23,000,000-24,000,000
1967	25,000,000
1968	26,000,000-27,000,000
1969	28,000,000-31,000,000
1970	32,000,000
1971	33,000,000
1972	34,000,000-35,000,000
1973	36,000,000-37,000,000
1974	38,000,000
1975	39,000,000
1977	40,000,000
1978	41,000,000
1979	42,000,000-43,000,000

Patek Philippe
1845	1,500
1850	4,000
1855	9,000
1860	16,000
1865	25,000
1870	35,000

1875	45,000
1880	55,000
1885	70,000
1890	85,000
1895	100,000
1900	115,000
1905	130,000
1910	170,000
1915	178,000
1920	185,000
1925	200,000

Peoria
1890	50,000
1895	75,000
1900	100,000

Rockford
1876	5,000
1877	15,000
1878	25,000
1879	35,000
1880	50,000
1881	60,000
1882	70,000
1883	80,000
1884	90,000
1885	100,000
1886	110,000
1887	125,000
1888	140,000
1889	150,000
1890	165,000
1891	175,000
1892	195,000
1993	200,000
1894	230,000
1895	260,000
1896	290,000
1897	320,000
1898	350,000
1899	385,000
1900	415,000
1901	450,000
1902	480,000
1903	515,000
1904	550,000
1905	580,000
1906	620,000
1907	650,000
1908	690,000
1909	730,000
1910	765,000
1911	820,000

1912	850,000
1913	880,000
1914	930,000
1915	1,000,000

Rolex

1926	28,000
1927	30,430
1928	32,960
1929	35,390
1930	37,820
1931	40,250
1932	42,680
1934	45,000
1935	63,000
1936	81,000
1937	99,000
1938	117,000
1939	135,000
1940	164,600
1941	194,200
1942	223,800
1943	253,400
1944	283,000
1945	348,100
1946	413,200
1947	478,300
1948	543,400
1949	608,500
1950	673,600
1951	738,700
1952	803,800
1953	868,900
1954	934,000
1955	1,012,000
1956	1,090,000
1957	1,168,000
1958	1,246,000
1959	1,324,000
1960	1,402,000
1961	1,480,000
1962	1,558,000
1963	1,636,000
1964	1,714,000
1965	1,792,000
1966	1,871,000
1967	2,163,900
1968	2,426,800
1969	2,689,700
1970	2,952,600
1971	3,215,500
1972	3,478,400
1973	3,741,300

1974	4,004,200
1975	4,267,100
1976	4,539,000
1977	5,006,000
1978	5,482,000
1979	5,958,000

Seth Thomas

1885	5,000
1886	10,000
1887	20,000
1888	50,000
1889	80,000
1890	110,000
1891	150,000
1892	175,000
1893	200,000
1894	240,000
1895	280,000
1896	330,000
1897	370,000
1898	420,000
1899	460,000
1900	500,000
1901	550,000
1902	600,000
1903	650,000
1904	710,000
1905	760,000
1906	820,000
1907	930,000
1908	1,055,000
1909	1,175,000
1910	1,325,000
1911	1,835,000
1912	2,355,000
1913	3,000,000
1914	3,600,000

South Bend Watch Co.

1903	300,000
1904	335,000
1905	360,000
1906	400,000
1907	445,000
1908	480,000
1909	520,000
1910	540,000
1911	590,000
1912	625,000
1913	650,000
1914	700,000
1915	730,000

1916	765,000
1917	800,000
1918	845,000
1919	880,000
1920	910,000
1921	930,000
1922	960,000
1923	980,000
1924	1,050,000
1925	1,100,000
1926	1,150,000
1927	1,200,000
1928	1,250,000
1929	1,300,000

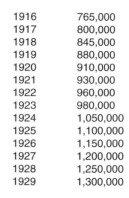

Trenton

1890	150,000
1895	500,000
1900	2,000,000
1905	2,500,000
1910	3,000,000
1915	3,500,000
1920	4,000,000

U. S. Marion

1870	40,000
1875	250,000

U.S. Watch Co. of Waltham

1887	3,000
1888	6,500
1889	10,000
1890	30,000
1891	60,000
1892	90,000
1893	150,000
1894	200,000
1895	250,000
1896	300,000
1897	350,000
1898	400,000
1899	500,000
1900	600,000
1901	700,000
1902	750,000
1903	800,000

Vacheron Constantin

1850	50,000
1890	180,000
1895	217,000
1900	255,000
1905	287,000
1910	330,000
1915	360,000
1920	390,000
1925	398,000
1930	405,000
1935	427,000
1940	450,000
1945	475,000
1950	500,000
1955	525,000
1960	550,000

Waltham (American Watch Co.)

1854	1,000
1857	5,000
1858	10,000
1859	15,000
1860	20,000
1861	25,000
1862	35,000
1863	45,000
1864	110,000
1865	180,000
1866	260,000
1867	330,000
1868	410,000
1869	460,000
1870	500,000
1871	540,000
1872	590,000
1873	680,000
1874	730,000
1875	810,000

1876	910,000
1877	1,000,000
1878	1,150,000
1879	1,350,000
1880	1,500,000
1881	1,670,000
1882	1,835,000
1883	2,000,000
1884	2,350,000
1885	2,650,000
1886	3,000,000
1887	3,400,000
1888	3,800,000
1889	4,200,000
1890	4,700,000
1891	5,200,000
1892	5,800,000
1893	6,300,000
1894	6,700,000
1895	7,100,000
1896	7,450,000
1897	8,100,000
1898	8,400,000
1899	9,000,000
1900	9,500,000
1901	10,200,000
1902	11,100,000
1903	12,100,000
1904	13,500,000
1905	14,300,000
1906	14,700,000
1907	15,500,000
1908	17,000,000
1909	17,600,000
1910	17,900,000
1911	18,100,000
1912	18,200,000
1913	18,900,000
1914	19,500,000
1915	20,000,000
1916	20,500,000
1917	20,900,000
1918	21,800,000
1919	22,500,000
1920	23,400,000
1921	23,900,000
1922	24,100,000
1923	24,300,000
1924	24,500,000
1926	25,200,000
1927	26,100,000
1928	26,400,000
1929	26,900,000
1930	27,100,000
1931	27,300,000
1932	27,550,000
1933	27,750,000
1934	28,100,000
1935	28,600,000
1936	29,100,000
1937	29,400,000
1938	29,750,000
1939	30,050,000
1940	30,250,000
1941	30,750,000
1942	31,050,000
1943	31,400,000
1944	31,700,000
1945	32,100,000
1946	32,350,000
1947	32,750,000
1948	33,100,000
1949	33,500,000

1950	33,560,000
1951	33,600,000
1952	33,700,000
1953	33,800,000
1954	34,100,000
1955	34,450,000
1956	34,700,000
1957	35,000,000

Waterbury

1880	100,000
1885	1,000,000
1890	3,000,000
1895	5,000,000
1900	7,500,000
1905	9,000,000
1910	12,000,000

Westclox

1905	4,000,000
1910	10,000,000
1915	18,000,000
1920	25,000,000
1925	37,000,000
1930	50,000,000

Glossary of Commonly Used Terms for the Vintage Watch Collector

Accutron: See "tuning fork watch."

Adjusted: A term referring to the temperature correction and positional timing of a movement. An adjusted watch usually refers to a high-grade movement which has been adjusted in five positions: dial up, dial down, pendant up, pendant right, pendant left for pocket watches, and dial up, dial down, pendant down, pendant right, pendant up for wrist watches. Also referred to in two temperatures—usually 42 degrees Fahrenheit (5.5 degrees Celsius) and 92 degrees Fahrenheit (33 degrees Celsius).

Alarm: A watch that can be set to produce an alarm sound at a predetermined time.

Analogue (Analog): Term used to denote any timepiece with dial and hands, as opposed to "digital display."

Arabic figures: Figures on a dial, such as 1, 2, 3, 4, as opposed to Roman numerals, such as I, II, III, IV.

Arbor: The axle of a wheel or a shaft that turns in a bearing; commonly referred to as the barrel arbor, pallet arbor, or winding arbor.

Automatic: A self-winding watch using a rotor or oscillating weight. Autowind.

A.W.I.: The American Watchmakers-Clockmakers Institute, a national watchmakers and clockmakers organization.

Balance: The oscillator, in the form of a wheel, which with a balance spring (hairspring) attached, is the time controller or governor of the watch escapement.

Barrel: The round box-like container in which the mainspring is coiled.

Barrel arbor: The axle of the barrel around which the mainspring is coiled.

Beat: The tick as an escape wheel tooth drops on to the locking face of the pallet. In beat means the correct rhythmical action of the escapement. Out of beat generally means an audible alternating light and heavy tick producing a halting, lame effect.

Bezel: The top part of a watchcase, a ring or frame that contains the crystal.

Bimetallic: Two dissimilar metals either fused or riveted together. In watches, brass and steel are usually used, as in the split balance wheel having a brass rim and steel frame to compensate for temperature changes.

Bow: That part of a watchcase to which a chain, etc., is attached; usually a circular ring pivoted into the pendant.

Breguet: Abraham Louis, 1747-1823, horological genius and inventor. The name applied to the type of hairspring which has its last outer coil raised above the body of the spring and curved inward.

Bridge: The upper plates in a watch movement that contain the bearings for the wheel pivots and have pillars at both ends, such as the train or barrel bridges. Also balance bridge (balance cock).

Caliber: The size or factory number of a watch movement.

Cannon pinion: A thin, steel tube with pinion leaves at its lower end and usually carrying the minute hand at its upper end.

Cap jewel: The flat, solid jewel upon which rests the pivot end. Also called the endstone.

Case: The container of a watch movement.

Case screw: Screws (usually two) that hold the watch movement securely in the case.

Center wheel: The wheel, usually in the center of the movement, to which the cannon pinion is attached. Also known as the second wheel.

Chronograph: A watch with hour and minute hand and a center sweep-second hand, which can be controlled by a special button. A watch where the second hand may be started, stopped, and made to return to zero. This is additional to the normal hour and minute hands indicating the time of day.

Chronometer: A watch or clock adjusted to keep exact time. In England, it is usually associated with the detent escapement as distinct from the lever escapement and was primarily made for the purpose of determining the longitude at sea. In Switzerland, a chronometer is a precision watch regulated in different positions and various temperatures, having obtained an official timing certificate.

Click: The pawl used to prevent the ratchet wheel from turning back after the mainspring has been wound.

Compensating balance: A bimetallic balance of brass and steel split near the arms and constructed so that its effective diameter will contract or expand in temperature changes to compensate for these changes to itself and to its hairspring.

Crown: The winding button on the top of the stem. The winder.

Crystal: Clear glass or plastic mounted into a watch bezel to protect the dial and hands.

Cylinder escapement: A type of escapement invented in England, which has no lever.

Damaskeening: Ornamental work on metal. In America, geometric designs and lines were etched into watch plates to increase their beauty. Damascene, from the word Damascus.

Demi-hunter: A watch with a half-hunter front cover. The half-hunter has a hole cut into the full hunter cover so that the hands can be observed without opening the cover.

Detent: The setting lever. Also that part of the chronometer escapement that locks the escape wheel. A detainer or pawl.

Dial: The face of a timepiece from which the time or other functions of the mechanism can be observed.

Dial train: The train of wheels under the dial which motivates the hands. The cannon pinion, hour wheel, minute wheel, and pinion.

Digital display: Any timepiece in which time is read with digits, in place of the conventional dial and hands. Figures, for example 12:45, display the time. On watches, this may be by a rotating disk, light-emitting diodes (LED), or liquid crystals (LCD).

Double roller: Two discs mounted on the balance staff, the smaller, crescented disc set above the larger which contains the impulse roller jewel.

Double sunk dial: A style of watch dial having the seconds dial and the center of the main dial sunk below the main dial surface.

Duplex escapement: A frictional escapement with sunburst-style escape wheel. The escape wheel gives direct impulse to the balance in alternate vibrations.

Ebauche: A term used by Swiss manufacturers to denote the raw movement without jewels, escapement, plating, or engraving. The ebauche manufacturers supply their ebauches to trade name importers in the U.S. and other countries who have them finished, jeweled, dialed, cased, etc., and engraved with their own (advertised) name brands.

Electric watch: A wrist watch which uses the electromagnetic principle to impart impulse to a (motor) balance.

Enamel: Enamel is glass composed of silica, red led, and potash. It is used to make watch dials and to embellish watchcases.

Endshake: The free up and down space of pivoted wheels or arbors in their bearings. Endwise freedom of movement of a staff, etc.

Escapement: That part of the mechanism of a watch which allows the power from the mainspring to escape. It consists of three main parts—the escape wheel, the pallet, and the balance.

Escape wheel: The last wheel in a watch train; it is the wheel which gives impulse to the controlling part of the mechanism, i.e., the balance.

Fourth wheel: Usually the wheel upon which is mounted the second hand.

Full plate: Refers to a watch movement design, the top plate of which covers the movement, the balance, and balance bridge (balance cock) being placed externally on the top of the plate; distinct from the 1/2 or 3/4 plate movements.

Fusee: The spirally grooved pulley of varying diameter used to equalize the pull of the mainspring. Used in early pocket watches.

Gold-filled: Like an Oreo cookie, a layer of gold, a layer of base metal, and then another layer of gold, all three fused together. Used for watchcases.

Hairspring: The spiraled spring attached to the balance to govern the speed of the balance oscillations.

Hack-watch: A watch with a hacking mechanism to stop the balance when the crown is pulled out, allowing one to synchronize their watch with other watches.

Horology: The science and study of time measurement.

Hour wheel: A flat brass, toothed wheel mounted on a tube which fits over the cannon pinion and supports the hour hand.

Hunting: A type of watch, usually a pocket watch case with front cover, which can be released and opened by depressing the crown and with stem-winding at the "3" position. Note: Always depress the crown when opening and closing a hunter case watch. Do not snap the cover closed as this will, over time, wear out the inside lip of the cover and result in a cover that will not stay closed.

Impulse pin: The roller jewel.

Incabloc: Trade name for a shock-resisting arrangement of balance jewels and staff design.

Isochronism: The quality of keeping equal time during normal runs of the mainspring, usually the qualities of a well-formed hairspring. When a watch keeps accurate time fully wound up, and at any period throughout its going until the mainspring is wound down, it is said to be isochronous (moving in equal time).

Lever: Usually referred to as the pallet.

Lever-set: A pocket watch in which a lever must be pulled out (located under the bezel) so that the hands can then be set by turning the crown.

Light-emitting-diode (LED): A digital time display made up of lighted bars or dots.

Ligne: A European unit used in the measurement of watch movements (1/12 of the French inch, or 2.256-mm).

Liquid Crystal Display (LCD): Extremely thin glass-liquid-glass sandwiches that can be made transparent or opaque by application of an electrical charge and thus be made to represent figures; a constant display, unlike LED.

Lugs: Horns extended from the watchcase to which the band or bracelet is attached.

Mainspring: The main or principal spring of a watch; the driving force, distinct from those which operate levers, etc.

Marine chronometer: A boxed watch clock set in gimbals utilizing the spring detent escapement; used on shipboard to determine longitude.

Minute repeater: A striking watch that will ring the time to the minute by a series of gongs activated by a plunger or push piece. A watch striking the hours, quarter hours, and additional minutes.

Minute wheel: The wheel in the dial train that connects the cannon pinion with the hour wheel.

Moon dial (moonphase): The dial carrying representations of the moon by which, in conjunction with an aperture in the main dial, the moon's phases are indicated.

Movement: A term used to denote the mechanism only of a watch.

NAWCC: The National Association of Watch and Clock Collectors, Inc. A national association of collectors with a few chapters overseas as well.

Niello: A form of semi-hard black enamel decoration used, as a rule, on silver watchcases.

Nonmagnetic: A balance and spring composed of alloys that will not retain magnetism after being put through a magnetic field.

NOS: New-old-stock. A watch that is old but that has never been used, and is usually in like-new condition.

Open face: An uncovered watch dial with the figure "12" at the winding stem—unlike a hunting style, which has a cover and winder at the "3" figure.

Overbanking: The malfunction of the pallet fork in which it shifts from one banking pin to the other without being released by the roller jewel.

Overcoil: The Breguet type of hairspring.

Pallet: The jeweled lever working in conjunction with the escape wheel; the frame containing the pallet jewels.

Pendant: That part of the watchcase to which the bow or ring is fitted. The position of the winding button (crown) is generally referred to as the pendant, especially for timing purposes.

Pillar plate: The lower or main plate of the watch.

Pin pallet: The lever escapement wherein the pallet has upright pins instead of horizontally set jewels. Used in non-jeweled cheaper watches. Pin lever.

Pinion: The small-geared arbor of a wheel pushed by a larger wheel.

Pivot: The thin end of a moving axle or arbor.

Plate: The frame of a watch is usually formed by two plates separated by pillars. The "train" etc., is pivoted between them.

Position timing: Adjusting a watch so that it keeps precise time when the watch is placed in a given position.

Quartz timepiece: An electronic watch or clock whose accuracy is controlled by the piezo-electric effect of a specially ground quartz crystal.

Regulator: Part of the balance bridge, which resembles a racquet (racket) and contains vertical pins, which straddle one coil of the hairspring. When the regulator moves toward the stud, the effective length of the hairspring is made longer and the balance slows in speed; when the pins are moved farther from the stud, the hairspring is made shorter and the watch goes faster.

Repeater: A watch that will ring the time when a push piece is motivated.

Repoussé: A decorative treatment of metal that is hammered or punched up from the reverse side to form a decoration or design when viewed from the face or front. Used on watchcases.

Rolled gold plate: A plate of base metal with a thin layer of gold on each side.

Roller jewel: The upright ruby pin set into the impulse roller.

Roller table: The impulse roller that the roller jewel is set into. It is fitted to the balance staff.

Rotor: The swinging weight in self-winding watches which turns fully in a complete arc of 360 degrees, as differentiated from the term "oscillating weight," whose arcs are restricted by bumpers.

Safety roller: The small, crescented roller disc placed above the impulse roller. The upper part of the double roller.

Setting lever: The detent, which fits into the slot of the stem and pushes down the clutch lever. Part of the winding and setting mechanism.

Single roller: A roller containing both the jewel and the safety crescent on one disc. Improved upon by the more modern double roller.

Size: American system for measurement of watch movements.

Spring bar: A spring-loaded pin that attaches the band or bracelet to a wrist watch.

Staff: A pivoted arbor or axle; usually referred to the axle of the balance as the "balance staff."

Stem: The squared shaft going through the winding pinion and clutch wheel on which one end is threaded to accept the crown.

Stopwatch: A simple form of chronograph with controlled starting and stopping of the hands.

Stopwork: The mechanism on the barrel of a watch that permits only the central portion of the mainspring to be wound, thus utilizing that portion of the spring whose power is less erratic. (Maltese cross Geneva stopworks).

Stud: The metal piece anchored to the balance bridge into which the outer end of the hairspring is attached.

Sunk seconds: The small second dial which is depressed to avoid the second hand from interfering with the progress of the hour and minute hands. Also referred to as the sub-seconds dial.

Third wheel: The train wheel between the center and fourth wheel.

Timing screws: Adjustable balance screws used to decrease or increase the effective diameter of the balance in order to retard or hasten its vibrations.

Tourbillion: A watch in which the escapement, mounted on a cage attached to the fourth pinion, revolves around the mounted and stationary fourth wheel. Invented by A. L. Breguet, its purpose is to overcome various vertical positional errors.

Train: A set of wheels geared or connected together. In a watch, these wheels are the center wheel, the third wheel, the fourth wheel, and the escape wheel.

Tuning-fork watch: Battery driven and tuning fork controlled. Invented by the Swiss and developed by the Bulova Watch Company of America (Bulova Accutron). In production by 1961, the timekeeping properties are extraordinarily good, but not as good as the quartz crystal watch developed in the later part of the 1960s.

Up-and-down indicator: A small subsidiary dial or separate indicator showing the extent to which a mainspring has been wound up or has run down. Also called reserve power indicator in automatic watches. Wind indicator.

Sources for Further Information

Resources
Contact author Dean Judy at:
Dean Judy
P.O. Box 1004
Rogue River, Oregon 97537
Web site: www.deanjudy.com
Email: info@deanjudy.com

Watch dealers:
Eric Iskin
Olde Towne Jewelers
125 Fourth St.
Santa Rosa, CA 95401
Phone: 707-577-8813
Email: oldetown@sonic.net

Bill Hegner
116 Woodland Drive
Scotts Valley, CA 95066
Phone: 408-354-8366
Email: ashwoof@cruzio.com

Rene Rondeau
Hamilton Electric Watch
Sales and Service
P.O. Box 391
Corte Madera, CA 94976-0391
Phone: 415-924-6534
Email: rene@hamiltonwristwatch.com
Web site: www.hamiltonwristwatch.com

John Noveske
P.O. Box 789
Grants Pass, OR 97528
Phone: 541-474-5547
Email: John@watchbuyer.com
Web site: www.watchbuyer.com

Organizations
American Watchmakers-Clockmakers
Institute, Inc.
701 Enterprise Drive
Harrison, OH 45030-1696
Phone: 513-367-9800
Fax: 513-367-1414
Web site: www.awi-net.org

National Association of Watch and
Clock Collectors, Inc.
514 Poplar St.
Columbia, PA 17512-2130
Phone: 717-684-8261
Web site: www.nawcc.org

There are many sources and suppliers
for watch materials, reference books,
parts, and watchmaker tools. The following are just some I have dealt with over
the years and from whom I have
received excellent service:

West Coast
Otto Frei & Jules Borel
P.O. Box 796
126 Second St.
Oakland, CA 94604
Phone: 800-772-3456
Fax: 800-900-3734
Web site: www.ofrei.com

Mid-West
CAS-KER Co.
2121 Spring Grove Ave.
P.O. Box 14069
Cincinnati, OH 45250-0069
Phone: 800-487-0408
Web site: www.casker.com

Jules Borel & Co.
1110 Grand Ave.
Kansas City, MO 64106
Phone: 800-776-6865

East Coast
S. LaRose Inc.
3223 Yanceyville St.
Greensboro, NC 27405
Phone: 336-621-1936
Web site: www.slarose.com

Watch-case repair
Wuischpard and Son
4644 N. Friday
Cocoa, FL 32926
Phone: 888-811-3934
Email: jpwish@msn.com

Custom-made pocket-watch crystals
Casadero Railroad Crystal Co.
Bill White
P.O. Box 188
Jenner, CA 95450
Phone: 707-865-1938

Watch Stuff
Buy-Sell-Trade
Online trading site for watches,
materials, and tools
Email: info@watchstuff.com
Web site: www.watchstuff.com

References
Catherine Cardinal, *The Watch, from Its
Origins to the XIX Century*, Wellfleet
Press.

Donald de Carle, *Watch & Clock
Encyclopedia*, N.A.G. Press.

Henry B. Fried, *The Watch Repairer's
Manual*, AWI Press.

Michael C. Harrold, *American
Watchmaking, A Technical History of the
American Watch Industry, 1850-1930*, a
supplement to the NAWCC Inc.

Rene Rondeau, *Hamilton Wrist Watches,
A Collector's Guide*.

Movado, Assouline Publishing Inc., 601
West 26th St., 18th floor, New York, NY
10001.